MICROAGGRESSIONS
Across the Great Divide

High-Stakes Written Assessments, the Threat of Stereotype and Hidden Curriculum

Mark A. Pierce

RoseDog Books
PITTSBURGH, PENNSYLVANIA 15222

The contents of this work including, but not limited to, the accuracy of events, people, and places depicted; opinions expressed; permission to use previously published materials included; and any advice given or actions advocated are solely the responsibility of the author, who assumes all liability for said work and indemnifies the publisher against any claims stemming from publication of the work.

The author has made all the requests necessary for a scholastic text in the form of a thesis from which the book originated. Materials from other writers have been properly cited. Any copyright discrepancies arising after publication will be addressed in subsequent editions.

All Rights Reserved
Copyright © 2011 by Mark A. Pierce
No part of this book may be reproduced or transmitted
in any form or by any means, electronic or mechanical,
including photocopying, recording, or by any information
storage and retrieval system without permission in
writing from the author.

ISBN: 978-1-4349-8304-6
eISBN: 978-1-4349-4549-5
Printed in the United States of America

First Printing

For more information or to order additional books, please contact:
RoseDog Books
701 Smithfield Street
Pittsburgh, Pennsylvania 15222
U.S.A.
1-800-834-1803
www.rosedogbookstore.com

TABLE OF CONTENTS

Table of Contents iii
Foreword .... vii - ix
Chapter 1: Discussing the Threat of Stereotype .... 1 - 6
Chapter 2: Perceptions and Passive/Aggression .... 7 - 19
Chapter 3: High-Stakes Barriers .... 20 - 27
Chapter 4: Repressive Learning Environments .... 28 - 39
Chapter 5: The Ebonics Debate .... 40 - 56
Chapter 6: Educator Demographics .... 57 - 60
Chapter 7: The Future of African American Education .... 61 - 64
Chapter 8: Student Voices .... 65 - 73
Chapter 9: Case Studies .... 74 - 81
Bibliography .... 83 - 88

To Corinne, my soul mate and friend who allows me to muse,
to my parents, August and Bessie Pierce, who taught me the
true meaning of the rewards sacrifice can bring, to my children,
Mark and Tiara, and my grandchildren, Xavier, Koko, and Aniah.
To my brothers and sisters who shared discoveries with me;
Lastly, this book is dedicated to Sharon Klein, Phd., who challenged
me insistently in order to make an idea become so much more than
opinion; she guided me to making it truth. I would also like to mention
the help and support of my publisher, and Martha Whitaker. Thank you
all for making this possibility become a reality.

FOREWORD

From someone on the front lines of education, and one who is there from a second career position, my research and studies have given me insights in how to make a paradigm shift in secondary school assessment, and in college recruitment, as well, that could close the achievement gap for our young people of color. A dialogue needs to be conducted about race, though, it seems, and there are ground rules and information that must be made known to all the parties involved in order to have a constructive discussion.

I am an Illinois native, born 65 miles southwest of Chicago. My father was a civil rights activist in that county at a time when grass roots thinking about human rights were not the norm. I wish my father could have lived to see this day. He formed an interracial council within my home town that got things done to bring all the citizens into a better accord with each other. I remember him being trapped in Chicago on the weekend of Dr. King's assassination, while he and my pregnant mother were attending a priorly arranged HUD conference to get much-needed housing for minorities in the town. My father and mother placed my seven sisters and brothers in the care of our family physician for that time and my wonder and amazement at the wealth I was embedded in soon wore thin. My ten year-old eyes saw how worried my father's friend was becoming when he went outside and would come back in to watch more news and await further phone calls.

I soon began to realize my parents were in mortal danger and that people were dying in Chicago. The good doctor offered to fly his personal plane up north to get my dad and mom, I found out years later, but my parents would have none of that. They waited in a church on the Southside, with all the rest of their group, until transportation could get each and every one of them safely out of the city.

The next week, in my fourth grade class, a little girl said aloud what she must have only overheard in her home. She said she was glad Dr. King was dead. "Now, maybe we'll get some peace around here!" she said. She didn't know my parents had faced men with guns in downtown Chicago, and were lucky to have gotten home safe. She didn't seem to even notice that I was the only black pupil in the class and was shocked into silence, much to my dismay, even now. But I could not choose to hate her; I only wanted her to like me. My pain was magnified because of the national trauma, but it was personal, too.

I've done things my father could never have dreamt about in his youth. My wife is German American and we have two adult children and a few grandchildren. Conflicted as our kids were, and probably still are, we always raised them to believe that they were very special. Because they came from the cosmic mingling of two very fine peoples and as Barack said, they cannot love one part of them more than the other. My wife and I aren't colorblind, of course, but we see the color of our skins supplanted by the unique promise of our love and character, and that makes the issue of our races a secondary thing. A very secondary thing, between us.

I am an assistant principal in an overwhelmingly white and Latino area. It is an area I lived in 20 years ago and experienced stinging racism in, while all the while surrounded by its bucolic grandeur. With the "audacity of hope" Barack extols, I believed I could return here to make this area my final home, and to help the brown and white children in my school celebrate life's brevity with an acknowledgment and reverence that only the true knowledge of possibilities can bring. And to make the best use of their time.

I am so pleased to be able to reach out to all my rainbow students, and to have them respond back to me in increasingly more and more authentic ways. They are talking about politics in ways that wash over the cynicism I'd heard forty years ago. They are ready for hope. Thank you, Barack, for helping me to reach them.

2008

* * *

Time passing has a way of tingeing our sentiments in ways that are aligned with synchronicities, sublime coincidences, and can leave you feeling cynical in spite of the capital of goodwill you may have had welled up inside of you, at one time. My previous foreword comments have somewhat of a hollow ring to the words, now, two and a half years later. I thought myself above being dragged down to unreasonable people's whims, but I stand corrected in that assessment. We, as African Americans, knew that having a Black president wasn't going to make things change overnight, but you did believe that now if you played by the rules and had done some bootstrap pulling, that you would have a place in the great society. Again, I was wrong on that assumption. I have not been offered employment as an administrator in the school district for the coming year.

We have a new superintendent, and he simply does not care to have me on the management dais, any longer, I'm told. He has found my "judgment to be suspect" after I began openly advocating for civil rights for African American students who were being harassed and discriminated against by other students. Some people would have called that being "uppity", I guess. I was not fired, just demoted, to a teaching position (a $50,000 pay cut). It is ironic on many levels, for me.

My hometown in Illinois was 16 miles from where Abraham Lincoln had his first debate in 1860. Ninety-eight years before I was born he stood at a familiar park in downtown Ottawa, and spoke mainly about Black Republicans (not the kind you are thinking of) and made some statements about what inalienable rights meant. Now, to hear President Obama, and others, you would say that Lincoln was on the vanguard of human rights. But on that day 150 years ago, Lincoln said he would not seek to free slaves; that Negroes were genetically inferior to Whites; that Negroes could never be intellectual equals to Whites; and that the only right they had was to earn money from their labor. Our new superintendent wouldn't even give me that much.

CHAPTER ONE
Discussing the Threat of Stereotype

I began this writing as a thesis, and I thought about what a thesis should be comprised of, taking into account that my first option in study, creative writing, was not granted me for various and sundry reasons. As a culminating experience, a thesis should be a celebratory exploration into a problem the student writing it wishes to address. It is to be about a problem where the theories and techniques taught to the graduates can be utilized in a representative body of work, and to thereby come up with a solution. For some matters, maybe all, that is a daunting task. In completing that writing the graduates will have shown that they have indeed achieved a higher learning. It is much easier to get a favorable subjective assessment, however, when the status quo line of thinking is replayed within the text of your answer. When you deliver what's expected. But that arguably is the antithesis of what rhetorical study is about.

It is somewhat odd that I "chose" a field of English that has structured argument as its core of instruction. It's odd because I've been popularly known to be somewhat of an abrogator, a peacemaker, as it were. It was me who would be the one urging compromise when disagreements grew heated. But I had also been reminded, sometime in my youth, that when there comes a time for disagreement, to choose my battles wisely, and not to tally up pyrrhic victories when a much larger battle had yet to be won. Still, and all, underneath my even-tempered visage, while I was growing up there were dragons I still felt needed slaying, and with whom I was willing to engage. Even today, they are monsters to me. Demons of self-doubt and isolation that occur each and every day in some degree or another. And if I do explore these areas do I risk finding that therein madness lies? This book, therefore, was a frightening proposition, in that sense.

As a rheterotician, I should be able to persuade you that these feelings are real for many who are like me, an American of African lineage. And I should be able to also convincingly explain that it is the duty of White America to own up to the privileges it enjoys over minorities. It is the privilege that comes from having a canon legitimize what one student can write creatively, but to another it says you cannot. This creates two dilemmas for me. I risk making the writing of my opinion become possibly more of a personal vendetta rather than a thoughtful literary investigation. And it also risks me being demonized as turning out to be some sort of a radical theorist, now run amok with a Master's Degree in one hand, and gaining yet another, by twisting the warp and woof of the literary theory he's learned. If only I could make it all trite and simple for me, this reason to write this book. I know that I need the satisfaction of an explanation as to why the educational system works the way it does in assessing African Americans in arguably different ways than what White Americans receive. Yet I cannot deny pain in doing so.

I've been taught that when trying to impart rhetorical skills, either on paper or on a speaker's podium that one must give great concern to not becoming over-emotional about their subject; that is if one wants to be taken seriously. To not do so connotes getting out of control, and exhibits a failure of deliberate thinking. Problems are solved with deliberate thinking, for the most part. Yet effectual change is hardly serendipitous. However, it has a tinge of predestined benefit when it is accomplished in a timely fashion and the change is welcomed. Now, even though change means progress, and progress never came without some expression, or manipulation, of radical thinking (something that is called for in a situation where a whole culture is being put to task, where a whole institution is being called upon for its accountability) it only seems fair to present a balanced approach in the argument. Not just hot rhetoric.

Communication in areas such as this, the places where wounds are raw, is too often bereft of such an understanding. I think it should be acknowledged here and now that the writer and reader must agree that they desire an understanding and that that understanding should be derived from there being a sense of satisfaction in the way a subject or topic is introduced. This willingness to understand therefore precludes any disagreement, or at least allows the seeming respect of agreeing to disagree. Rhetoric, I've found then, is more about finding agreement between dissimilar points of view, rather than discovering points of continual conflict and argument. We learn when we see all sides in pursuing change for the better, but rhetoric is the medium that pulls back the branches of entrenchment so that one can then see the sky of reason.

In a 1996 article in *Higher Education* (Vol. 21, Issue 1) a researcher places student performance accountability upon the teacher, as well as the student. The piece illustrates how much personal satisfaction is needed for "effective learning" to take place. Written by Janet Donald, she abridges herself to the heart of my subject matter by saying that academicians frequently gloss over the fact that a student needs to like what they are studying, and not just the act of studying, itself, in order to perform better. "Evaluating Undergraduate Education: The Use of Broad Indicators" says that "Given the considerable investment of time and energy most students make in attending college ... [it]

suggests that their perceptions of the value of their experience should be given substantial weight and that student satisfaction cannot be legitimately subordinated to any other educational outcome (23)." In the end, that student should be able to say that the outcome was worth all the tribulation because they now have a degree and can earn a better livelihood. But philosophical inconsistencies discovered in that pursuit taint it.

One of the reasons I wholeheartedly believe that contextual matriculation, teaching framed within the context of knowledge a student possesses (e.g. scaffolding), is one of the keys needed to having effective learning taking place is because a student is validated within the frames of reference in the curriculum when this process is used. In whatever the subject matter, connections must be made with the realities of the one doing the learning. There needs to be some self-actualization occurring, to where the student sees themselves characterized fairly in the representative work and that they have been regarded equally. In subjective courses, those in the schools of liberal studies, that is not the case and it affects student attitudes about the curriculum. Donald and her co-author, Brian Denison, however, talk about the "characteristics" that students should or should not have upon entering a place of higher education and they would have us believe that subjective traits prior to enrollment in college are negligible factors in assessing the satisfaction of a student, and in turn, their performance. They do not seem to take into much of an account what ethnically marginalized students go through prior to and upon entering colleges in America. Their frame of reference is askew to the subject's reality.

I oppose this supposition because I clearly see as how self-perception (a subjective analysis) makes a marked difference in people's values, and in their level of personal fulfillment, regardless of their station in life. And while it's true that this often goes across lines of color, and may include class issues, it would be redoubtable to say that a person could speak to how satisfied they are with their education, after the fact, if they could never envision what they were potentially prior to being trained (Horjortsji 13). This is the true barometer of intelligence. It would be erroneous of investigators to negate these personal evaluations to a lowly substratum within the making of their findings. It is true that you get out what you pour in, and there is another saying that follows that line of thinking, as well, "They won't care to know if they know you don't care." Though mnemonic in its sentiment, from that saying it's expressed that it is only reasonable to assume that if you feel that you are not wanted by the taskmaster, pleasing the taskmaster can then become an arduous journey for any student, and the faint of heart will not pick up the yoke placed before them. The question remains, however, as to whether teachers should be "burdened" with making their students "like" them; and not only them, but also like what they are teaching them. Are teachers distinct entities in the classroom, separate from the curriculum they teach, or are they a conduit to acquiring and indelibly linking to the process of learning?

The answer is, of course, they are at times both; in some instances more so often than others. The more salient thing to keep in mind, however, is to perhaps ask whether or not it should be incumbent upon students to always please the teacher, or to in some way, somehow, get satisfaction (for the work that they will do) all by themselves. A student may expend a tremendous amount of effort to do well in class and assignments, but yet they may still find themselves given a less than satisfactory return on their efforts. They may well receive a lower assessment even though they followed the assignment rubric, or followed the analysis modality that was required of any other student. However, the instructor places a lower grade on their paper because they have personal aversion to the writer. This is especially true for many African American students throughout the country, and especially more the case here, in California. How can a student be satisfied with a situation like that? Why is it the popularly held belief that California is the most liberal state in America when in Harvard's *Civil Rights Project* it says that California is the fourth most scholastically segregated state in the union (Orfield 26)? Another source says that African American placement in secondary AP English nationwide is half that of Whites (Freel 17), and yet another says Blacks are more likely to be designated for remediation in high school and that ability grouping is probably racially imbalanced in highly integrated schools (Jencks 336).

How can there be such a disparity between two groups of peoples? The reason that matters so much is self-evident when the legacy of the country is considered, but why is it that the color of person's complexion is such a divisive subject? It seems that class and race are so inextricably linked as to what is actually valued in the conscious mind of most people in America, that whether they want it to be or not, the debate cannot be avoided. An analysis of something called stereotype threat may help to explain how class and race are intertwined in the process of discriminatory teaching. The threat of stereotype isn't a disease, but it is symptomatic of a harassing, "bullying" trauma that can numb the survivor into becoming polarized, and then maybe even giving up thinking that they are capable of being considered intelligent—or maybe even becoming intelligent.

The Threat of Stereotype

In "Thin Ice", a 1999 three-part Stanford study, Claude M. Steele wrote about the phenomenon I've been describing. Steele argues that socioeconomics is not the main factor for Blacks performing poorly in post-secondary schools. He notes that because solidly middle class African American students consistently have "lower standardized test scores, lower college grades, and lower graduation rates" that something else must be operating beyond class distinction in a society that claims to have achieved equality in education. "My colleagues and I have called such features 'stereotype threat,'" Steele continues, "the threat of being viewed through the lens of a negative stereotype, or the fear of doing something that would inadvertently confirm that stereotype (49)." This fear is often activated by some oblique comment or response that both surprises and aggravates the target, which is usually unprepared for the disparagement coming their way. They are victim to being lulled into a false sense of security, complacent about their racial identity ever being demonized because after all, they are in a scholarly environment. The slight(s) catches them quite unawares and shakes the psyche of the African American student, and his or her confidence.

Students who feel stereotype threat choose to disengage rather than suffer. As Steele notes, "We have called this psychic adjustment 'disidentification.' Ceasing to identify with the part of life in which the pain occurs often lessens the pain and this withdrawal of psychic investment. This departure may be supported by other members of the stereotype threatened group—even to the point of it becoming a group norm. But the danger in not caring can mean also not being motivated. And this can have real costs. When stereotype threat affects school life, disidentification is a high price that groups contending with powerful negative stereotypes about their abilities—women in advanced math, African Americans in all academic areas—may too often pay (49)."

Whites too can feel the effects of stereotype threat when they participate in actions, mannerisms, or activities of an "out" culture; they can feel it when they may be dancing or otherwise performing in front of African Americans or Latinos; Zora Neale Hurston said that, "It is the lack of symmetry which makes Negro dancing so difficult for white dancers to learn" (Leitch 1150); or it could be that the unease can be felt in interracial dating situations, or whenever they are outnumbered by minorities. They most assuredly feel it when they believe they are assumed to be racist when they don't believe they have reason to be. The uneasiness that exists in varying degrees beneath the surface of that predicament can cause guilt or anger, and sometimes a combination of both. It's a thing that many White people just can't grasp: the fact that white skin tone provides access to better things.

Author Tim Wise, a political activist, believes that Whites tend to see things in a quantitative, rather than qualitative slant. One example he gives is when recently town officials in Cedar Rapids, Iowa thought it would be a good thing to have African Americans represented in the town fabric. Welcoming ads were bought in newspapers where Black populations centers are established, places like Chicago, Milwaukee, and St. Louis. And not surprisingly, few takers were found, even though jobs, housing, and good schools were promised. Those African Americans who did relocate were treated to a rude awakening, however. The city fathers in all their configuring had not disseminated to citizens, police, or businesses that emigrant Blacks were coming to town and that they were supposed to be welcomed. The vision therefore failed, rather quickly and miserably, and the naysayers had ready blame to place on the Blacks who came to town instead of the planning failures of inept, well-meaning liberals. The townspeople attracted the subjects they wanted, but had no idea as to what supports would be needed to help sustain a viable quality of life for the newcomers. They were treated in ways that Blacks had been customarily treated in most parts of the Midwest because the mindset of the dominant culture could not interpret Blacks in any other way but the iconic ones they'd been raised to believe in.

Is what was just described passive racism or is it racist at all, for that matter? Wasn't the intention of the town elders to give Blacks an opportunity that they wouldn't normally get? Was the opportunity given them good enough to serve the purpose of attempting to reach out in brotherhood, or did their success require something more? And if so, why couldn't it have been given to them? Tim Wise is astounded that the Black experience is never legitimized until someone who is White signs off on things told to them countless times by Blacks. "It's a matter of privilege," he says.

"I was a nineteen year-old white boy from Louisiana who wanted to go to Tulane University and didn't have a pot to piss in. My family was just this side of poor, and I was great at procrastinating with turning in the forms for financial aid." Because of his poor management, Wise found himself $10,000 shy of the costs needed to attend. "We didn't have money, but my late grandfather had some property. Down in the poorer area. An area where Blacks huddled together to make places to live. My grandmother, without a second thought, went down to that bank and put up one of those houses for collateral to finance my education. So, my livelihood, as it is, all came about because of the privilege I had of being from a family that made money out of keeping Blacks down. And I got that. And that's when I vowed to use every bit of what education I received to eradicate that condition (21 Jan. 2006)." The Cedar Rapids Integration Committee could not give urban Blacks access to White privilege like Wise had received, and even if the newcomers had had money, proprietors still reserved the right to pick and choose who they wished to do business with. Blacks faced with integration of this kind consistently have been expected to acculturate to the culture of power, but not to assimilate into it.

To put this in parallel with education, it is similar to what happened in America's colleges and universities when Blacks were to have been given access to higher academia. One might be allowed to enter the hallowed halls, but efforts to make the interloper feel welcomed could not be legislated. More so in the past, but even presently today, Black college students in English curriculums are felt to be castigated when they raise objection as to how their history and story is portrayed in the fiction of the country's White authors. Like the Black 20th century settlers in Cedar Rapids, they were told that they would be welcomed and given every opportunity afforded to them under the law, but the hearts and minds of the citizenry, and in this book's case, the scholars, could not be made to accept them or their agenda, if they did not care to give any value to either.

CHAPTER TWO
Perceptions and Passive Aggression

In a college English course I took in 1990, I was marked down once on an essay where I was discussing Melville's *Benito Cereno*. The American Literature professor, a man in his early 40's, instructed my class to write an analysis of one of three short novels we had read. The only other specifics to the writing were to be that we had to reference our observations about the story with direct quotes and citation from the book. I don't recall what the other stories were, but I do remember that *Benito Cereno* was the only one that resonated with me because it was the only story that gave an opportunity to consider a Black man's interpretation on Melville's romantic and realist twist.

Set in the 18th century, the story was about a merchant ship which comes to the aid of another which has run aground on a coral reef. Among its cargo were a number of slaves who propped up a hostage captain to appear as if he still had control of them and the ship. I expounded on the point that it was more than likely that the White characters underestimated the slaves due to cultural perceptions. I juxtaposed an alternative ending, as I was encouraged to do in another class by another of my professors. My instructor for this class, however, gave me a "C" and reprimanded me for considering the text from an African American viewpoint, preferring the analysis to be colorblind in its essence.

His comments were to the effect that I did not follow directions and had no business trying to reconfigure a masterwork. This response, I now know, totally works against what would be a valid literary analysis of the work, and worthy of higher assessment for its extended use of metacognition, and innovative thinking. After all, this was a lower division class, and the thinking presented was above standard, more so than just a plot line's reconstruction and commentary. And yes, I would acquiesce that the professor had a reason for being subjective as to whether or not he got an adequate response, but my work was not without relevance. It seemed my opinion about the text was antithetical, and inferior, to the closure he desired and expected. I have found that this was not unusual for college students to have happen to them at that time, however:

> In the 1980s, in the field of composition, postructrualist understanding of reading and writing, and of their interconnection, produced electrifying innovative curricula. The destabilizing force poststructrualism exerted on canonicity, intentionality, reader's function, and reader's relationship to writer, text, and context, would make it possible, and even imperative, for some teachers and scholars in certain pockets of English studies (especially composition and women's studies) to validate and to study novice readers' steps toward interpretation (Helmers 197).

I brought an ungraded copy of the essay to the former professor who generally was responsive to most of my writing and he believed it to be insightful work, but he could not get his colleague to reconsider the grade. It seemed to me that the professor had taken a personal attack at me, rather than just my work, but here again; I gain further solace from Marguerite Helmers:

> Orally as well as in writing, I had been schooled to recite: I had been taught to interpret what I read by weaving together…the interpretations of established scholars. My 'own' interpretation, as those of my classmates, did not count: they had no place in scholarly discussions of the canto, nor could they be the subject matter of writing, my own, and even less, my teacher's. I am not trying to demonize my teacher. I am suggesting, instead, that in light of the dominant theories of reading in circulation…at the time, she could not frame my 'difficulty' as anything other than the result of my inadequate preparation, or of my irrelevant, arrogant, preposterous 'response' (197).

This then was exactly what my experience had been, but experienced by a White woman in Italy. This illustrates how gender and discrimination are closely paired. Women collectively are an even larger minority than African Americans and Helmers recounting is shadowed by my own. Yet, she did not feel her teacher to be a misogynist, but that is typical. Christopher Jencks says, "Students seem to understand the distinctions of status that these behaviors convey…blacks are more affected by teacher perceptions than whites, and more represented among students of whom teachers expect less (342)." My professor was irritated for my not citing scholarly sources for my opinion, but rather trying to inveigh my personal insights into an interpretation, and he did not seem to like the fact that I was bucking his pre-conception of my abilities. The threat of stereotype therefore kicked in for me after that one experience. I took the reprimand from him at a personal level and thereafter began to disidentify with the class and the instructor. My final grade for the class was a "C" and only one of two I ever received in both my undergraduate and graduate English course work.

Hardships, it seems then, can come about from the perceptions students have about their instructors in all their educational endeavors. This speaks as to whether the teacher feels the student is a high-achiever or a low-achiever, where the teacher will be "criticizing them more often for failure...praising them less often for success...calling on them less often for questions...monitoring and structuring their activities more closely; *in grading tests and assignments, not giving them the benefit of the doubt*... (Jencks 340-342). Jencks also infers that to complicate matters, as is often the case, modern discriminatory practices are so thoroughly embedded that they are virtually invisible.

It could be argued that the historical bias about everyone and everything that connotes being African American still stands in the way of English educators giving minority material they read an objective, or as much as it can be objective, academic assessment, "There is empirically based evidence of teacher bias against black students, and it is obvious that listeners may not limit their criteria for judgment strictly to quantifiable data. Furthermore, if students are labeled as less capable and are then treated as such, they will probably begin to display characteristics of those who indeed are less capable" (Winsboro 52). And, more crucially, it is often too difficult for these same individuals to see that there are biases at work around them, or to understand why African Americans might feel deeply resentful of the margins set for them in institutional settings. Even college teachers who feel that they are giving equal opportunity to all their students can still be found to have misplaced agenda in their evaluations. It is difficult for them because they are simply ambivalent to race, and to their identity as a White person, "Ambivalence theory...holds that Whites simultaneously hold both negative and positive attitudes toward Blacks and that attitudinal ambivalence results in polarized attitudes towards Blacks. Thus, in our sample, it might have been that Whites who exhibited the most ambivalence...also held the most racist attitudes (Juby 9)."

Juby formed her study about White racial identity attitudes using J.E. Helms 1984 data and research where he designates five statuses (stages) that Whites use to "interpret and respond to racial cues." *Contact* is an attitude that denies race being meaningful in their own life, or in society; *Disintegration* is marked by confusion in the roles that Whites use in socializing, where the individual might sublimate their racial identity to consider minority rights; *Reintegration* is the 'innate belief' of White superiority and pride in one being White; and *Autonomy* is where Whites have a non-racist alignment with other Whites.

It is the racial cues that these divergent Whites use to interpret Blacks that place African Americans into the margins of the paper in the American book of justice and prosperity. These kinds of margins are based on how a person looks, and the things that they may do or say. The boundaries of these margins overlap into all areas of culture, but none are so essential to livelihood as English studies. The challenges provoked by these perceptions are not aberrant but consistently exist from kindergarten through graduate school for many African Americans, and the disparity is especially noticeable when they have similar educations and backgrounds with Whites who will still end up performing better in assessments, or in finishing college at twice the rate of their Black high school peers. This may be simply explained as the effect of a self-fulfilling prophecy narrated to Blacks over the centuries in a master narrative adopted by the canon. Content bias; therefore, can be a fuel of combustibility within many of the conceptions alluded to about the African American student. The de facto belief system maintains that they are not seen as equals within the classroom at many levels of matriculation.

College teachers can be oblivious of the fact that they are thinking about their African American students in ways that are biased, as Juby and Helms said, but much of that bias comes from their being so ensconced in the class culture of White America that it isn't even noticed by them, or their students, who come from the culture of power:

> It is a common, if controversial assumption that teachers' perceptions, expectations, and behaviors are biased by racial stereotypes…For example, Sara Lawrence Lightfoot writes: 'Teachers, like all of us, use the dimensions of class, race, sex, ethnicity to bring order to their perception of the classroom environment. Rather than teachers gaining more in-depth and holistic understanding of the child, with the passage of time teachers' perceptions become increasingly stereotyped and children become hardened caricatures of an initially discriminatory vision" (Jencks 274).

Other studies besides Helms' have also been conducted to analyze the amount of race neutrality a teacher may have and seemed to also confirm that teachers are racially biased whether it's known to them, or not. "In experimental studies researchers systematically manipulate information about students…the sample is selected to avoid any correlation between race and the other characteristics noted," Jencks said, "teachers receive information about students in written descriptions, photographs, videotapes—or occasionally, real children…the teachers then predict one or more measures of ability or academic performance for each student. If the experiment is run well, the teachers do not discern that race is a variable… or that the real purpose is to assess their racial biases (276)." What is it that White people see when they look at Blacks is the question.

Ralph Ellison wrote in 1953 that Hemingway once said that all American literature evolves out of Mark Twain. In his essay "Twentieth Century Fiction and the Black Mask of Humanity" Ellison surprisingly extols Huckleberry Finn as a humanist work that illustrates the zeitgeist of that time period: the conflict of human rights over property rights, but he maligns Faulkner's,

Steinbeck's, and Hemingway's more in depth, but just as unrealistic, set of archetypes (Mitchell 135-139). These characters are so cemented within our civilization that they have the impact of an ideology. Firstly, there is the *Sambo*, a complacent man-child, then comes the *Mammy*, the usurper of power in the Black family; the *Uncle*, an obedient double agent; the *Coon*, a razor wielding thug or a buffoon like dandy, the *Pickaninny*, a bestial progeny of the lower forms of humanity, and last but not least, as was already mentioned, *The Black Brute*, a rapist (Riggs 1987). These icons, singularly and in conjunction with one another, can cause overt actions to come about that are discriminatory and stereotyped amongst a diversified population

The Sambo, Mammy, and the Uncle all are inventions from a patriarchal time in America when antebellum slavery was the rule and it was believed that slavery was good. The Sambo didn't care if he was deprived of citizenship as long as he got fed and got physical comfort; the Mammy was a strong defender of the White work ethic and the one to demand it of all family members, not the father (if one was present); and the Uncle represented a Booker T. Washington ideology of belief that separate but equal is fine for the majority of Blacks. The images that come up in the popular culture of that time shows grinning faces and uniforms of service beneath polished bronze visages of subservience. These were the archetypal "Good Negroes" and were not to be feared.

And simultaneously working as a double-edge were the visions of immoral Negro brutes who you couldn't rationalize with if they became frustrated, or you grew exasperated with if you tried to do business with them. These were the predecessors to the kind of Blacks that a century and a half later Malcolm X would call the "Other Brothers", and they were what awaited America, he said, if it didn't capitulate to the desires of Martin Luther King, Jr. and grant Blacks equality. These were the ones who would take what they felt they deserved, or didn't. They were punishing Negroes who sought an eye for an eye. All characterizations of African Americans have been derivations of these popular icons associated to the race. What is wrong with these stereotypes is that they are all easily overlooked because they are based on witnessed peculiarities that are in some aspects factual to most people. To a very small extent, these traits and behaviors are then expanded upon and exploited in the stereotype to present a semiotic representation of Blacks that will resonate culturally and commercially. But let us predate Twain's catalog and examine the first works of fiction in America to root out a hypothesis that furthers my theory.

Here is how American English literature has depicted Americans of African descent from the very first, and began the creation of the cues, or ethnic notions that Whites came to associate to Blacks: Washington Irving wrote this first fictional account of a "Negro" in his story "The Legend of Sleepy Hollow". In this scene, the character of Ichabod Crane is daydreaming in the school house when his reverie is disrupted:

It was suddenly interrupted by the appearance of a Negro, in towcloth jacket and trowsers, a round-crowned fragment of a hat, like the cap of Mercury, and mounted on the back of a ragged wild, half-broken colt, which he managed with a rope by way of a halter. He came cluttering up to the school door with an invitation to Ichabod to attend a merry-making or 'quilting frolic,' to be held...having delivered his message with that air of importance and effort at fine language, which a Negro is apt to display on petty embassies of the kind, he dashed over the brook, and was seen scampering away up the hollow, full of the importance and hurry of his mission (McMichael 629)."

There would be some readers who would say that this excerpt brings African Americans to the comparison to a god-like being; the illusion to Mercury and the ability to tame a wild horse can be seen as enviable attributes. But then juxtapose that to what Irving says about what happens commonly when a Negro is communicating to their betters. He wrote that the Negro had: *that air of importance and effort at fine language, which a Negro is apt to display on petty embassies of the kind*. What is this implying?

Well, firstly, it is all too telling that Irving is saying that language is a gauge of value, and that African Americans are seen, at best, as only capable of mimicry. The feral associations connected to the slave or freedman, are exploited and adhered to in the characterization, but the Negro is not endowed with even simple intelligence. Washington Irving is using the "coon" caricature, here. A coon was a popular contrivance in media at one time, used to portray freedmen as miserable failures and contributing greatly to the race debate of the time (Riggs 1987).

Early vaudevillian venues would commonly have blackface comics assault the standard dialect of speaking in minstrel shows. Audiences delighted in the effort expended by these comedians, who went through all sorts of verbal contrivances trying to make them selves be understood. So, the Washington Irving depiction is the first literary image of an African American cemented into one of the first, if not *the* first American Romantic story. And though the attempt to being understood is acknowledged, Irving says that Negroes tend to only code switch this way when they are doing the bidding of a White, one who has told the Negro what to say. Irving is saying the Negro is not capable of the rhetorical skills needed to say anything of consequence through his own processing. It is an assertion of prototypical humanity, if it is to believed.

Then he has the Negro scurrying around like an uncaged monkey: *he dashed over the brook, and was seen scampering away up the hollow*. Western culture has rooted this conception into its psyche firmly. One 16th century legend said that the Negro race actually came about through the hybridization of ape and man; European travelers had come across the first Negroes they had ever seen and then "the most man-like of the apes simultaneously." Winthrop Jordan says that the connotations fueled judgments. Fifty years later, a theory called the Chain of Being would even more firmly imbue African Americans with bestiality:

> The tendency to associate the two flowed in part from certain presuppositions…The chance tales of travelers interlocked with the concept of the Chain of Being to transform the fortuitous geographical proximity of Negroes and apes into an association of cosmic significance…Almost certainly that fortuitous proximity played a crucial role in shaping the eighteenth century consensus on the Great Scale of Beings [that] the place just above the ape was occupied by the Negro (Jordan 229)".

Given that this kind of ideologue was being entrenched in the White culture of the time, for almost two hundred years, or more, it's surely not implausible to understand why Washington Irving's Negro character should be able to ride a half-trained horse.

And it should also be noted that Irving eradicates that sense of separateness and storytelling between the author and his reader and brings the reader into sharing the narrator's thoughts and perceptions; it is then that another racist marker can be seen to exist in the work. Irving, through the narrator, confides to the reader about a tendency he notices in listening to Blacks speak, something that is evidently quite common to him. He is sharing his personal beliefs with the reader who is patently taken to be White. He has the narrator talk about how common it is to see Negroes putting on airs of importance, something equals would say to one another when talking about supposed lesser-men. That motif of innuendo mixed with its social revelations is devastating in attacking Black freedom. It attacks the very basis of being human, actually, which is inherently, the ability to be able to communicate.

But a motif is not truly a motif unless it repeats itself within a narrative. Irving remains consistent here and thereby employs the character of an "Uncle", playing a fiddle, "accompanying every movement of the bow with a motion of the head; bowing to the ground, and stamping with his foot whenever fresh couples were to start" (McMichael 632). And he also added sambos and pickaninnies: "Ichabod prided himself upon his dancing as much as upon his vocal powers. Not a limb, not a fibre about him was idle…He was the admiration of all the Negroes; who, having gathered, of all ages and sizes, from the farm and the neighborhood, stood forming a pyramid of shining black faces at every door and window, gazing with delight at the scene, rolling their white eye-balls, and showing grinning rows of ivory from ear to ear" (McMichael 632). It should be noted that Walt Disney seemed to leave out these blatant images from his animated version, however. Disney and Irving both seemed to be saying, centuries apart from one another that: Negroes are inconsequential in the telling of a story except as devices. But that is not to let Mr. Disney's company off the hook. Arnett in his 1992 study found that

Disney animators and directors used dialect and accents to build character stereotypes:

> Especially in more recent years, Disney has engaged African American actors to provide the voices of major characters in their animated films...Perhaps more disturbing than the issue of human versus animal form is the way in the world which is cast so clearly for those African Americans who are speakers of AAVE. The stereotypes are intact; the male characters seem to be unemployed or show no purpose in life beyond the making of music and pleasing themselves, and this is as true for the crows in Dumbo as it is for the orangutan King Louie and his crew of primate subjects in the *Jungle Book*. Much has been made of King Louie and his manipulation of the only human being in this story...he convinces his audience that he has one goal in life, and that is to be the one thing he is not: a human being, a man. African American males who are not linguistically assimilated to the sociolinguistic norms of a middle and colorless United States are allowed very few possibilities in life, but they are allowed to want those things they don't have and can't be (Arnett 93-94)

African American literature has as one of its tropes the figurative masking of its characters, characters who assume identities alternative to who they really are. It makes for the ability to obtain things they would not normally be privileged to partake of. The masks have variations of need and motivation depending on what is desired. It is part of the trickster motif and was used in 19th century African American novels such as *Chloe* and *Iola Leroy*. The authors of these works, however, did not merely dramatize the Black experience for a story. In revealing how the deceptions played out they also revealed the actual coping device that Blacks use when pressed to exist. It has been used in our education, as well. It happened for me every time I read and reread *"The Adventures of Huckleberry Finn* in school. While reading it aloud in class, and listening to my White classmates read it, I put on my mask and acted like I thought it was a great adventure, but cringing inside. And that is what keeps many Blacks from falling in love with the canon, because its truths are disproportionate to our realities, and therefore not having the power to radically change it, we wear masks. When you are maligned in literature you put up a mask in front of your face that allows you to still read the canon, but knowing in your heart of hearts while doing so that there is a division of otherness that will always place you outside of its privilege. African American literature taught me another thing, quite well, and again something that I already knew. And what I learned was that of all the adjectives associated with the Black experience that I had read, privilege was not one of them.

Tim Wise mentioned a funny thing about the semantics of the word "privilege". I happened to have my laptop in my possession on the night I heard him speak in Hollywood. Wise said that the ease of writing today has become so technologically driven that it sometimes belies our deepest intents. Remember, as I implied earlier, the perception of what is communicated is what really matters. Wise said that if you're writing a paper on a computer using Microsoft Word you can type in the word PRIVILEGE in lowercase font and nothing will alert you that there is something grammatically wrong with that word. So, that's what I did. I typed in PRIVILEGE and what he said was true. Then Wise said to also type UNDERPRIVILEGE, and nothing will be flagged there, either. But when you type the word OVERPRIVILEGE there should be a red line that shows up under the bottom of the word. And that line is telling you that the word is improper. There is something wrong with that word. Privilege means to have freedom, license, opportunity, dispensation, advantage, benefit, concession, right, honor, pleasure, joy. If you are underprivileged you have less or none of these gifts. What is wrong with the word *overprivilege* is there is no such thing, you either are privileged, or you aren't. When you are underprivileged, however, you literally are *under* privilege. I reiterate my point here, that when you are maligned in literature you put up a mask that allows you to still read the canon, or whatever text put in front of you, but you also know in your heart of hearts there is a division of otherness that will always place you outside of privilege.

Once I used to consider what it would be like if Whites could put up as much an effort in getting into a historically Black college, as Blacks do trying to get into mainstream four year universities. If there were significant numbers of Whites trying to gain admission to Howard, Spellman, or Grambling, et al., as there are Blacks trying to get into Harvard, Yale, and Stanford, I would tend to believe that a condition of parity in education had come into existence. But we know that this is far from being true.

Truth is at the crux of what any subject finds desirable for analysis because the representations of what may be deemed a reality can be philosophically and theoretically shredded, rhetorically manipulated to such a degree that truth is perceptibly obscured. Through a process of separation, truth can become untruth, the opposite of truth, itself. Anglo American literary influence over the aesthetic and application of theory to African American narrative and criticism can be duly criticized, much as would be the argument for bringing an afro-centric ideology to all Western secular opinion. But, In New Historical terms, the filtering of African American societal and literary representation through an eyepiece of historic colonization can be materially argued as being motivated by politics, and it can also be said that such manipulation therefore makes the product inauthentic, to say the very least:

> The popular arts in the United States during the eighteenth and nineteenth centuries, as well as reflecting political and gender bias, also projected racist attitudes. As pointed out in William Van Deburg's *Slavery and Race in American Populist Culture* (1984), the popular arts in the United States 'record a great deal about the cultural underpinnings of American opinion on matters of race and slavery' (Soitos xi).

At a gut level, therefore, the images that represented blacks from antebellum time, until even today, are gross mischaracterizations, fomented from the practiced tropes of White authors and publishers. The society involved in this, one where Whites dominated, vacillated from portraying the American Negro as either a feeble illiterate, a comical figure, or as just so many sub-cultured brutes, depending upon the political climate of the time. A documented history exists of hundreds of insensitive approbations. What behooves the African American writer, and reader, from producing and/or reading a work of literature that is inauthentic as to their identity? Is offensive manipulation of ethnicity acceptable, as in the case of where appeasement of the masses overrides the needs of a veritable and positive cultural aesthetic for the minority?

In their 1949 essay "The Affective Fallacy," William Wimsatt and Monroe Beardsley perhaps *unintentionally* assist substantiating the premise of the nationalistic African American critics, that semantic substance is more important than form. Though these men were New Critical formalists, they posited that the understanding a person gets from a text is not equal to its effect, and they do not shrink from discussing the emotion elicited from the effect of the text:

> A question about the relation of language to objects of emotion is a shadow and index of another question, about the cognitive status of emotions themselves. It is an entirely consistent cultural phenomenon that...one kind of anthropology has delivered a parallel attack upon the relation of the objects themselves to emotions, or more specifically, upon the constancy of their relations through the times and places of human societies (Leitch 1391).

What was quoted, I believe, seems to speak in explaining the need and intent to relegate African Americans to a cultural second-class by White society throughout the centuries, and it maintains that it is an emotional agenda based on politics. Race has always engendered strong feelings within literature, and more specifically American literature, and African Americans have been sorely objectified throughout the canon. The dehumanizing elements in the stereotypes contained in the canon's body import meaning (Helm's cues) by the relation of the object to the emotional response it brings out, it stands to reason then that it is imperative that the objects of subjective thinking be responded to more favorably, more inclusively, within academia.

I believe to really understand the dimensions of this polemic, one has need to momentarily examine the layers of Western culture and its effect in the relation to the matriculation of African Americans. As first registered in the beginning of this piece, there is a political dynamic as to what constitutes the attitudes of literature about the Black race. This literature dictates curriculum used in all schools of thought, and has an implied double meaning emanating from its teachings. This "hidden curriculum" is patriarchal and thus favors

White males. Structuralists would cite the philosopher C.S. Peirce as to explain how the stereotypes of images become entrenched.

He said that the semantics comes about through a divergence of three different signs: the icon, the indices, and the symbolic. The icon is a sign that in some way resembles the thing it stands for; the index stands for a thing that can be associated to the sign; and the symbolic represents a rule of understanding about the sign's meaning (Eagleton 87-88). There are laws of understanding, or symbolics, which are associated with these signs regarding African Americans.

For the *icon* you can input any of the seven stereotypes previously mentioned. The *index*, the things associated with these images are: laziness, gluttony, baseness, immorality, lasciviousness, simple-mindedness, etc. The mission of this hidden curriculum is to affect a continued White advantage. It rewrites, or suppresses historical points that it feels does not serve the purpose of preserving the ideals of democracy that were, and are, based on a patently racist supposition.

Now, I don't believe they do this intentionally, but indirectly they do. The supposition that I am referring to says that the collateral and residual exploitation of the seed of the sons and daughters of former slaves is not a reprehensible thing. In fact, it is only logical to assume that such an ideology it is to be required if White self-interest is to be preserved. In some respects it is not unlike some aspects of Nazism. It arguably has been accountable for providing the creation of a mass of wealth from the original forced servitude; and a subsequent cash cow that has also been created from the accrual of criminal justice revenue (when taken into account the percentage of Blacks fined and/or incarcerated to their population) from fines and incarcerations.

The thinking is a rather elementary one; failing to keep Blacks under a system that allowed money to be made from their free labor, the society has found a way to transcendentally subsidize itself for that loss, in the machinations of the court system. The longer subjugated individuals are kept (or deemed to be) ignorant, the easier it is to continue this system of economical subterfuge; but given a collective knowledge, the oppressed can then only be divested for a short time longer before the inequitable politics becomes transparent to all. Keeping a group ignorant, therefore, in order to produce a yoke of direct or indirect servitude is all that is needed. If the subjects are made to believe that their lot in life is not meant to be any better, if they are held to the lowest standard of achievement before even being given a chance to try, they will continue to walk in the rut around the grinding mill of poverty and despair, and barely be given time to eat the mud underneath their feet.

I saw this every time when African American students at my former high school laughed at the idea of them ever enrolling in an advanced studies course. According to Friedrich Nietzsche, the subject's role in aesthetic judgment (their idea of being able to transcend) is marginal, controlled by the nobility of the art's (concepts) creator, who uses the weaknesses of the human intellect, and its lack of discipline, to misrepresent truth. Nietzsche said, "Human beings allow themselves to be lied to in dreams every night of their lives, without their moral sense ever seeking to prevent this happening, whereas it is said that some people have even eliminated snoring by willpower (Lietch 875)." It seems to me that this could be what Janet Donald meant, theoretically, when she cited sources who believe a student's subjective viewpoint outside of the classroom has nothing to do with their classroom satisfaction. And yet, the classroom is a microcosm of a macrocosm that the student exists in; the two are inextricably linked. A worldview such as this, where one sees the bigger picture, is crucial in forming one's self-identity.

In way of explanation, Marx's forerunner, Hegel, also posited that there are two distinct classes of subjects whom evaluate aesthetic judgment, each with their own roles of behavior and rationalization, the master and the slave. As a subject, the master can appreciate the artistry of deception, while the slave moralists are bowled over by the pandering made to their base nature. And how that permeates culture. I think every African American might want to have the privilege of Whites, and their encouragement. But along with the acknowledgement there should also be some retention of their own, stated Black Identity, or the master narrative suborning the "ennobled" slave.

The contrary to this is the acknowledgement that if Whites are to maintain the status quo they now enjoy there must be a restriction put in place to keep such socioeconomic parity from ever coming into fruition. Education thus serves as the gatekeeper for the access to privilege because, as the saying goes, knowledge is power. That is why it was against the law to teach slaves to read and write (Appiah xii), or to allow Blacks to pantomime, or to in any way have them communicate to one another other than in the most common of public utterances. This is why it was so pivotal a challenge to desegregate the nation's schools. That is the ultimate and most powerful tool of racism. And one would be surprised to hear the myriad definitions of racism.

Racism, as I understand it, is having the privilege or the power to grant or deny someone a thing they need, based on their color, and it is truly aligned with that oppression when people are being mandated from learning about themselves, subjectively, in relation to the world around them. Judith Katz says in her book *White Awareness* that racism can be defined as: 1) A belief that human races have distinctive characteristics that determine their respective cultures, usually involving the idea of one's own race is superior and has the right to rule others; 2) A policy of enforcing such asserted right; 3) A system of government and society based upon it; 4) Perpetuation of belief in the superiority of the White race, and 5) Prejudice plus power (51).

There is arguably yet a class system that is two-tiered and entrenched, stacked against African Americans ever proportionally attaining the accoutrements of power enjoyed by White society. The system propagating this ideology makes the African American an object instead of a subjective being with purpose and self-determination. Karl Marx's "product of labour" premise stated that the more complexity one inputs into an objective form (in this case, the present literary tradition and its images) the more of it is lost. African

American intellectuals writing in forms that maintain the status quo hierarchy of Western thought (about Black people) therefore lessen themselves, and because some critics, such as poststructuralists, maintain that the author does not speak for himself, but for their collective culture, these writers then lessen the identities of all African Americans. Marx characterized the hegemony as a kind of self-loathing:

> The *alienation* of the worker in his product means not only that his labour becomes an object, an external existence, but that it exists *outside him*, independently, as something alien to him, and that it becomes a power of its own confronting him; it means that the life which he has conferred on the object confronts him as something hostile and alien (Leitch 765).

These perceptions are received early on by African American young people and the association continues, unfortunately for far too many, until the day they die. And it is this system of arrested cultural development, and stymied views, that are affecting their acclimation to the nurturing potential of academic writing, and to its societal acceptance.

It therefore leaves many feeling that having an education doesn't guarantee that you'll do any better for yourself, materially. All things being equal (though they are not) these students see that there are easier ways to make money (though not as much) and less wasteful ways (though not as productive) to spend their time, rather than going to college; and they may figure that if they're only going to be treated in such a prescribed fashion, regardless of teaching or lack thereof, they redirect their energies elsewhere.

Numbers tend to back up this observation. Proportionately, though Blacks and Whites have parity in completing high school, they show a greater disparity in their ability to complete getting a higher education (The Condition of Education 2000). It was found that though only five percent more Whites (88%) than Blacks (83%) get their high school diplomas, slightly less than half of the numbers of Blacks end up graduating from college: 25% compared to 12% (Freel 17).

Laurence Steinberg, Sanford Dornsbusch, and Bradford Brown completed a study twenty years ago in California and Wisconsin, both places of which I'm familiar, and interviewed 15,000 students of different races about antiachievement norms in their culture, and they reported, "These African-American youngsters, we learned from our interviews, find it much more difficult to join a peer group that encourages the same goal (academic success). Our interviews with high-achieving African-American students indicated that peer support for academic success is so limited that many successful African-American students eschew contact with other African-American students and affiliate primarily with students from other ethnic groups" (Jencks 380).

CHAPTER THREE

High-Stakes Barriers

According to the 2000 census statistics, there are approximately 296,500,000 Americans and of those millions, 81% (243,130,000) are Anglo and 13% (32,000,000) are African American. The Census Bureau says that the differences in the rate of high school completion between African Americans and Whites narrowed in the 25 to 29 year-old age range over the last decade of the Twentieth century. By 1997 it was found that the completion rates in these two groups were virtually identical in proportion to their demographics. Statistically, at that time, it could be verified that the field was level based on performance through high school. But that has changed. It was reported on NBC News on April 1, 2008 that though Whites maintained a 78% graduation rate, Blacks, however, fell back another 25%—to 53% total graduates. 47% of African American high school students do not graduate in America during that period. This falls in line with the disparity in postsecondary achievement reported earlier, where it was stated that half of the African American students who graduate from high school go on to complete college.

High school graduates who go on to graduate from a four-year college have the potential to earn $600,000 more during their lifetimes than their counterparts who do not. Furthermore, they will earn approximately a million dollars more than a high school dropout. This should then beg the question as to why the importance of attaining a post-secondary education is generally looked down upon by many Black students. Even with the information just related, and the related health opportunities coming from being educated, even if with all of that—only 24% of the country has at least an associate degree. This past year's California High School Exit Exam (2007 CAHSEE) revealed that though African American students performed better in a statewide comparison (improving their subgroup performance by 4.7%);

urban school district averages where Blacks attended were anywhere from 7 to 11 percent lower than the city and state levels mandated by the State Board of Education.

Socioeconomics and class restrictions, notwithstanding, and despite the accoutrements of financial aid and affirmative action, African Americans, in liberal studies especially, seem to fall to the wayside and drop out of college, if not even failing to enroll in the first place. Yet many Whites believe that African Americans have reached the promised land of equality. And that analysis is derived from the racial identity of the objector and their interpretation of what it takes to exist as a marginal citizen in America. This could possibly be from a shift in high-stakes testing criteria from elementary schools to high schools. Results from the testing seems to indicate that test-based accountability systems are used more for adjusting curriculum than shoring up student deficits in a direct manner, especially in the lower grades where the fundamentals should be learned. "Certainly testing that creates 'gates' through which students must pass in order to be promoted will lead to an increase in retention in grade…Grade retention has increased in recent years, particularly for African-American students" (Hamilton 98). Teachers of these students reallocated their curriculum focus with these students and begin "teaching to the test". In Arizona it was found that the amount of class time spent on test preparation and test administration was greater in urban, low-income, high-minority districts, and only high academic expectations were considered for high-achievers because of high-stakes testing (99). This effectively locked out African American students from getting the higher skills in reading and writing needed to go to college because they had no in-depth study being given to them to prepare for that. And while it was intended to make education more equitable by having test-based accountability, general trends seem to show that it does not accomplish that.

Tim Wise reported that 6% of White Americans (14.5 million) believed that the affects of discrimination were negligible in present-day America, and that no further remedies are needed to counter institutionalized slights. But to put this in a truer retrospective, he added, one must also know that twice that number of Whites also believe that Elvis Presley is still alive. In another recorded remark in a newspaper, Wise found that 75% of Whites claimed to have "many" Black friends. He points out that many means several, or more than a few. The number five would seem to fit this meaning, he said: three would be a few, and four, minimally, would mean more than a few. In an instance of largesse, therefore, Wise gave a benefit of doubt to the pollsters and said that each of these Whites has five Black friends. If this is true, 75% of White Americans (222,375,000) count each African American seven times over as a personal friend (Wise 2006). With such goodwill it seems implausible that Blacks don't do better when it comes to matriculating after high school, and this, as has already been shared, is not the case. But what is the expected performance for freshman college students regardless of race? The American College Testing Service found in a 1995 survey that even in the most selective schools 14 percent of freshmen stop, or go on hiatus from studies, by the start of their sophomore year (Hjhortshoj 3).

This means both White and Black have problems adjusting. That is consistent with the parity these races have in high school graduation rates. But the reason that less than half of the Black graduates go on to college may be that many of them had been given inflated grades in inner city campuses to socially promote them out of the school system (Freel 18). This left them with a high school diploma in their possession but little skill to show for it. And in that context Hjhortshoj also writes that notwithstanding the fact that students who have weak high school backgrounds often do extremely well in college, some advanced students find it quite difficult to negotiate the requirements of undergraduate studies because they were not given opportunity to learn and nurture salient skills: the diversified types of reading, writing, and thinking required in the beginning undergraduate studies (3). What he does not conjecture, however, is the comparative statistic for advanced college students who matriculate, and the remedial students he mentions.

In both cases, to be sure, there must be a transcendence of sorts in what any student writes for a class between what was expected in high school and now demanded in college. That is the point where a student learns to write to the purpose of a paper desired by their college teacher (Hjhortshoj 3), but in doing so also feels that the performance will be judged with an unbiased and fair eye. Instructors' assessments should, therefore, not be biased towards a student's work based on labels, content, methodology or predictions, says Christopher Jencks (83). They should judge how well the student summarizes, compares, analyzes, synthesizes, argues, criticizes, interprets, proposes, and reports. Now, put all those requisites as elements in a high stakes essay that must be written in order to place a student into English 101 and the dilemma clearly presents itself. At the moment that blue book is opened to write the writer's proficiency exam, over a half-million dollars of potential earnings is on the line.

Students, of course, should know how to do all these things by the time they finish high school, anyway; and most will be capable of such if they have included honors or AP literature classes in their curriculum, but that is not the case for many African American students. Many of them come from a household where the language skills of the parents are at a deficit in comparison to Whites in their age group. "The Peabody Picture Vocabulary Test (PPVT)", says Christopher Jencks "tries to measure the size of an individual's English vocabulary. A word is read aloud and the subject chooses a picture that approximates the word's meaning." He found that the percentages between the groups were statistically insignificant, but it was still evident that Black children didn't know words comparatively well as their peers of the same age group, who were White. They were several years behind the Whites, in fact. "Black children, in other words, never catch up, however, so black adults know fewer words than white adults and these findings suggest that Black and

White English differ more in their pronunciation and syntax than in their vocabulary" (Jencks 67-68).

> The main reason why blacks score lower than whites on these tests is probably that black children have fewer opportunities and incentives to expand their vocabulary…Culture is not merely a body of knowledge and skills. It is also a set of strategies for dealing with the unknown and with tasks that seem difficult (Swidler). Culture can effect (sic) people's willingness to think about unfamiliar questions, their strategies for seeking answers that are not obvious, their motivation to persist in the face of frustration, their confidence that such persistence will be rewarded, and their interest in figuring out what the tester thinks is the right answer (Jencks 68-69).

Black people, therefore, who are racially isolated in areas where it is not necessary to converse and interact amongst Whites on a daily basis probably will not be initially adaptable to the system presented to them unless given a chance to prove themselves, and to grow acclimated to its designs. Their culture has different perceptions, motivations, agenda, and resources. Removed so far from the mainstream, they are self-contained communities, though deficient in socioeconomic ways, and operating under a different set of assumptions. These assumptions are based on "a priori" knowledge of White culture that is pervasive in everything around them and they know that linking themselves to that has never been edifying.

> White students do not criticize one another for 'acting white,' but they have many other derogatory terms for classmates who work 'too hard.' Blacks stigmatize effort in racial terms whereas whites do so in other ways, and one cannot predict a priori which form of stigma will be most effective. When we try to do this using the National Education Longitudinal Study (NELS), we find little difference between typical black and white students and only moderate differences between the top black and white students. In sum, our results do not support the belief that group differences in peer attitudes account for the black-white gap in educational achievement. In contrast, disparities in the family backgrounds of blacks and whites do account for the modest differences in effort that we find between the average black and white students. Policymakers, therefore, should not allow concern about the so-called oppositional culture to distract them from more fundamental issues, such as improving schools and providing adequate motivation, support, and guidance for students weighed down by the burdens of poverty" (Jencks 392).

This returns to chapter two's inquiry's about privilege. It falls along the line of a somewhat socialist philosophy, but nonetheless one accepted as a common belief in America, and that is, if one is privileged to customarily think they will receive fair and just dispensation for their efforts, they will then perform their work with a self-assuredness that produces good outcomes. But if that persistence isn't rewarded generationally, as it may be related by the parent to their child about their own experiences; if they are made to feel that dogged determination will not suffice in satisfying a certain college teacher's edicts, that student will likely not succeed. Some Whites may counter this argument and say that you can try and try, and try—try all you want to; but if the substance isn't there in the first place to succeed, it is a losing proposition to begin with. And if that is the case, then the boot-strap pulling ethos we have been raised to believe is an American fallacy, or at the very least a contradiction in terms. When that hardworking Black student can't be given the time to produce a breadth of work that would show their persistence in playing the odds in college assessments has produced some dividend, they will either not be allowed to be retained in higher education (by the litmus of academic probation) or they will quit altogether. What else speaks to, or explains, the dilemma of having half as many Black college graduates as Whites when comparatively the same proportions of each race graduate from high school? Or, if they are matriculated, they may not be afforded access to all the options within their chosen field of study. For the moment, however let us examine what standards of assessment are used.

Beginning with programs for basic writing, there are assessments used to determine placement in core instruction: English, Math, Science, and Social Studies. To redact the remediation policies of the past, the National Council of Teachers of English (NCTE), and its policy arm, the Conference on College Composition and Communication (CCCC) created a position statement on writing assessment (1997). The problem was that post-secondary campuses could not afford to hire faculty to go over retrieval-and-retention of basic writing skills that should have been mastered already by high school graduates. The general principles of this policy state that written assessment for high stake credits (such as high school graduation and college entrance testing) should be made up of several published texts from the student, not an incidentally timed writing from a prompt. The committee found that the latter kind of testing worked against students of diversity and succeeded in keeping many minority students out of college. The committee felt that if giving a timed response to an essay prompt is the method chosen for assessment, then they want the prompt to be relevant to contexts that are familiar to the student so that they will be motivated to respond to "listeners and readers in their environment." This requirement could easily be done in the framework of English 101 classes, but students working with multiple learning deficits were seen as pushing the case for lowering credit standards for those classes.

Limited funds were being spent on them going over basics when instructors generally felt that, frankly, that money could have gone to others who were better prepared and had solid basic freshman knowledge. And yet, Peter Dow Adams found that students who enrolled in first-year composition, but had been placed in basic writing, did better than students who did not take the basics course and then went on to freshman composition (Adams 30). The committee also found that timed writings (and their do-or-die criteria) were a disadvantage to the fair testing of minority students because they tend to be judged more on the relative number of surface errors rather than on content. This method works against minority writers because it penalizes them for sometimes writing in a style that reflects their speech, which for some may be African American Vernacular English. This form is labeled as "incorrect," typically, and distracts the reader evaluators.

There are, of course, strong disapprovals about disengaging from having any entry assessments involved in college registration. The true conservatives tend to lash out against that movement and feel that there is an elitist group of liberal pedagogues who have lost touch with the reality of a classroom. In this majority opinion, the conservatives interestingly call the reformers elitists. Those teachers insist on keeping the placement assessments as policy and they call those leaning to the modification or dismissal of the testing as being "new abolitionists" (a term hearkening back to the days of the American apartheid). They also feel that if high standards aren't mandated, these elitists are now the ones who will have aided and abetted, criminal inference intended, the stunting of the majority's *and* the minority student's education.

I had a chance to be supervising a student body meeting with juniors at my former high school where a guest speaker inquired about how prepared the students were to beginning to apply for college admissions. He asked if they'd taken PSAT tests and about half raised their hands; then he asked how many had taken honors or AP English, and less than a quarter did so. I didn't notice any African American students arms uplifted. Though more than a few laughed sheepishly at one another, as if they knew that was not something within the realm of possibility for them. A 1992 Time magazine article written by Sophronia Scott Gregory had a tag line in it that illustrates how these African American students may have bought-in to the mindset that they are not capable of showing intelligence. A sidebar in it said, "Talented black students find that one of the most insidious obstacles to achievement comes from a surprising source: their own peers" (Jencks 329). But the White students knew how important those classes were, and most had made progress towards lining themselves up for postsecondary placement. I could sense by the demeanor of many the African Americans, however, that were not as concerned, unfortunately. They had not even had the chance to write a college assessment, and they had already pulled themselves out of the equation to do better for themselves.

At that same former high school of mine, one that has won the Los Angeles Academic Decathlon for two years, and two national championships, there are no African Americans who have taken an Advanced Placement Literature class in the same time span, if not longer. In the past I encouraged one parent to seek Advanced Placement for their child, and had another seek my assistance in trying to get their child enrolled in it. But many African

American students and their families don't realize the importance of the class. If they come from a family that has had one or more members attend college, then they are more likely to be aware of this prerequisite and probably have taken steps to ensure that matriculation. But as was explained earlier, if there is a socioeconomic divide because of disparate educational experience at the home, many won't know to avail themselves of such opportunities, or be capable of negotiating their demands. If the societal barriers of economics and politics are not sufficient enough in gentrifying the gifted hallways, then several procedural hoops are instilled in the process to further impede the Black student and their family to gain inclusion. This is done supposedly for the sake of rigor. The following list represents the requirements for entry into AP classes:

1. Students must have attended or are presently attending a magnet school
2. Prior two semesters' GPA must be a 3.0
3. Students must have a special ability in the arts or be otherwise gifted
4. Standardized testing must show high percentiles across breadth
5. Student must be referred by faculty

Earlier interventions and opportunities should have been utilized from kindergarten to the 4th grade to ameliorate what the potential Black students needed to have groomed into them in order to be referred to advanced placement. But instead of placing them in bridge and magnet programs these youngsters were invariably assigned to learning tracks of low-achievers. Jencks quotes an 11 year old African American boy's assessment of his educational status. "The only thing that matters in my life is school, and there they think I'm dumb and always will be. I'm starting to think they're right. Hell, I know they put all the Black kids together in one group if they can, but that doesn't make any difference either. I'm still dumb…Upper tracks? Man, when do you think I see *those* kids? If I ever walked into one of their rooms, they'd throw me out before the teacher even came in. They'd say I'd only be holding them back from their learning" (Braddock and Slavin 51). In an effort to counterbalance the inequity, non-inclusion, and lack of cultural responsiveness, some high schools have opted to have open enrollment in advanced placement (AP) classes.

El Camino Real High School in Woodland Hills, California has such a situation. They operate their advanced placement program under the theory of immersion which is the principle behind second language acquisition (students are believed to rise to the level of the proficient students). In fact, what is puzzling about this is that though immersion is how many foreign language programs are conducted, yet when it comes to advanced placement, the pedagogy used for such acquisition is found wanting. Without such openness, these classes then form homogeneity, and then elitist considerations seem to be driving the opportunity behind whether or not the necessary prerequisites for postsecondary education are being equally disseminated.

Placement in such classes is seemingly guarded assiduously by many gatekeepers in the administration, faculty, and counseling offices of most high schools. And wherever a referral is necessitated, there is always the risk that a policy of nepotism, cronyism, or bigotry will determine those who will be eligible. Those who fall outside this favor will be left to fend for themselves as best they can. That, however, is not the end-all and be-all for Black students seeking higher education. As was the case with the Black Des Moines emigrants fitting into all categories but one can leave you without support. What is the predicament for those who have the socioeconomic base but are found lacking in hereditary wherewithal to find postsecondary placement? For them, as the saying goes, getting there is only half the battle.

I found by reviewing my own undergraduate and graduate transcripts that it is not until graduate studies, actually, that the African American student of English has the chance to explore, in-depth and expressively, self-determining literature, and even then there is a fight to be heard. So, acknowledge that, and admit there is a delayed gratification for them. The problem then has to be that they must firstly attain the baccalaureate before they can entertain joining that battle over the authenticity of what literature says about them.

In the primary stages of their college terms, English students will, of necessity, be relegated to becoming totally familiar with British and American literature, in both classical and neo-classical theory, and then their modern derivations. That, as has already been delineated in the first chapter, has been loaded with courses that have a particularly patriarchal and oppressive tone. The isolation that Black students feel in classes is almost palpable at times to them. "Being an African-American in these (English) classes is like being in a 'white boys' club'. There has never been one day when I have not felt like I am getting in the way of the class and teacher 'being themselves,' commented a female CSUN graduate student who happens to also be a teacher. Thus isolated, what behooves the African American student to retain their place in the pursuit of academia?

Regardless of the materials used, or the resources offered, it is a fact that "As students and teachers immerse themselves in the routine of schooling, perceptions and expectations both reflect and determine the goals; the skills, energy, and other resources they use to implement the strategies; and the rewards they expect from making the effort (Jencks 274)." Yet and still there are quite a few teachers who continue to believe discrimination has nothing to do with the dropout rate from colleges. To them it's as pragmatic as sifting chaff from the wheat without regard as to how the product withered because teachers, especially in college, don't have the luxury of time or the patience to get everyone up to speed. It is the leavening of such motivation that can make the difference for at-risk students. Black students feel that the teachers don't want to help.

CHAPTER FOUR
Repressive Learning Environments

In the previous three chapters the problem of the threat of stereotype was elucidated; and there are actually two points of contention within it. First, the barriers placed against African American college applicants by high stakes assessments don't really take into account what socioeconomic or cultural hindrances the candidates encounter, and secondly, there is no recourse given for the effect that certain teachers and their curriculums have upon African American students who sense that they are not appreciated or treated with the human dignity they deserve, simply because they are Black. The forthcoming chapters now will go into what comprises the environment that perpetuates the slight of stereotype threat.

The elements that go into that turmoil, I believe, happen to deal with some of the demographics attributed to the ranks of teachers; the ethnic notions Whites have about Blacks, the concerns about requiring standard English assessments (the Ebonics Debate), the devaluation of multiculturalism, the employment projections in education, the affirmative action backlash, and the commencement of the re-segregation of California schools in the inner cities all are again, part and parcel of the contention. Let us look into a modern sketch of this predicament, which arguably could be called a polemic.

I once worked in a high school where less than 17% of the entire school population was Black, more than 23% were Hispanic and the rest were White, yet a recent survey of students had a commentator claim that 60% of the school was made up of bused in minority students. In addition, the responder also inferred that "I believe until the rebuilding of the socio-economic structure of this city, that busing students in should have much more severe requirements. Hopefully this will change the fact that T___ has some of the brightest students, but receives the lowest test scores." Another also said that the school should "get rid of bussed in students". This student actually seems to be recounting what was said earlier about what the negative aspects are of test-based accountability systems. And he was not the only one to strike such a tone.

He and other students magnify the sentiments they hear not only from one another, but from their teachers, and if not from them, from their parents. When it was announced at a T___ staff meeting that the bussed population would probably be deferred to city sites in the coming year, there was more than a little smattering of applause from the faculty. The desires and dreams of the local antagonists at the school should be realized for what they are; "the severe requirements" the student called for may be an ignorant and limited understanding about the NCLB legislation. He is saying he wants the gates to the communities schools closed to those who do not pass academic muster, in his view, and those are students who come from the urban areas of Los Angeles.

No Child Left Behind was meant to reform and support the integration programs installed in education during the '70s to shore up the deficits in achievement that busing alone failed to do. By test-based accountability systems standards, it requires that all major ethnic groups and any subgroups, reach norms of standardized levels of state configured assessments. The level, however, is not denoted by correct answers, but by attendance. It is more important that the number of students exposed to the testing is met rather whether or not they pass the exam. 95% of each ethnicity must be present, and test, throughout the California Standards Test period. If that goal is not attained for three years in a row and targeted growth not shown, a school or district may be placed under program improvement status, and the receivership of the state takes over curriculum and budgeting. It also takes the school out of the loop for inclusion in the court-ordered district integration program (busing) because the opportunity of diversity cannot be balanced by the failure of resources and support given to minority students in "non-performing" schools. Failing that, I believe the displeased student seems to feel that there should be a policy to extricate the non-responsive minority groups from the campus. Under program improvement status, that eventuality would come to pass and, as Hamilton discovered, high-achievers scores will rise. But that student is not really concerned about Blacks and Hispanics bringing the schools test scores down because if he was he'd encourage those two groups to continue to bottom out, and then freed of that anchor the remaining majority students would then be able to show progress, and also that busing is a failure. What the complaining student really is insisting upon is that he does not want Blacks and Hispanics to be in such large numbers at the school because they, directly and indirectly, make him uncomfortable.

Fortuitously, in a bittersweet way, there are several new high schools coming on line in the city, and that is where T___'s non-indigenous Blacks and Latinos will eventually go. And there will be little or no interactions with Whites then. Will the disbursement of stereotype threat increase theirs or the Whites performance that will be left homogeneously in the San Fernando

Valley? Interestingly enough, the year prior to the decline of African American scores, it was the White students who failed to meet academic levels per capita and placed the school on program improvement status.

And if the answer to the former question is a foregone conclusion, what is it that makes up these tests that makes passing difficult for African American students? The content of these examinations and their specifications are made to reflect standards arrived at by experts on curricular content, in other words, teachers. From those having bachelors to doctorate degrees, it was the teachers who wrote the content standards and came up with the formative and summative assessments for the exams, though commercial exams do not per se have any state's particular standards in mind when they are being made. Laura Hamilton found that "Because tests are samples from a content domain, they may omit or poorly represent some important aspects of the larger domain. This failure to capture the entire domain is called *construct underrepresentation*. If a test fails to capture important elements of the domain, scores can only justify narrow or qualified conclusions about performance" (62). If you couple the negative form of construct underrepresentation with content bias, then there cannot possibly be a realistic appraisal given for any student, but that especially would be the case for any student of color. African American and White students therefore, both apparently, find it unreasonable to take a week of time for testing that doesn't have any relevance to raising their GPA; but now with high school exit exams factored in, what was taken lightly before is now a serious endeavor. Blacks, however, have something additional working against them in taking these tests, besides the normal teenage angst; they do not receive the same quality of education as their White counterparts do, being in the same school, or not. Standardized test scores are used, rightly or wrongly, to funnel deficient students into various remedial programs (Freel 18).

In these classes, curricular activity is designed around such activities as template handouts, a lot of videos, and educational games, or things of that nature. That is hardly a platform to instill rigor or to enhance learning, but that is what a lot of these remedial classes are like and the students recognize that they are on a low-achiever track. Frustrated therefore, by past failure and discompassionate teaching, the students act out, and then their teachers are more than willing to cast out of the class. It could be called the "Untouchable Syndrome".

Given that it is understood that there generally are deficits in the class of students who happen to be African American, why would a teacher refuse to let such a student stay in their class, in spite of moderate behavior problems? I believe the answer is in the case study comment where the student overemphasized the number of students who are bused. African American students are culturally known to be loud and aggressive; and this is not to be seen as being bigoted insight, or something embittered with any self-loathing, Zora Neale Hurston said it herself in her critical essay "Characteristics of Negro Expression":

It is said that Negroes keep nothing secret, that they have no reserve. This ought not to seem strange when one considers that we are an outdoor people accustomed to communal life. Add this to all-permeating drama and you have the explanation. There is no privacy in an African village. Loves, fights, possessions are, to misquote Woodrow Wilson, 'Open disagreements openly arrived at.' The community is given the benefit of a good fight as well as a good wedding. An audience is a necessary part of any drama. We merely go with nature rather than against it" (Leitch 1153).

And that truth being demonstrated in a classroom can be a very discomfiting thing for a teacher that has had little to no experience with Blacks, and even for some of those who have. The problem conceived seems larger than it actually is because the perception of what is happening is based upon cultural rules and messages about Blacks. In reality, for these Whites, being around African Americans who are assertive or aggressive makes them nervous, extremely so.

Sarah Sentilles was a volunteer in the Teach America program in 1995. In her book, *Taught by America: A Story of Struggle and Hope in Compton*, Sentilles gave a candid report on what a White teacher feels when encountering the threat of stereotype in a neighborhood and its schools. I'm going to put in an entire interview written by David Ruenzel of *Teacher Magazine* because it is compelling and illustrative:

> Q: *Was teaching in Compton a lot harder than you expected?*
> A: Absolutely. I think that it was something I wanted to say that I'd done, but not something I actually wanted to do. This was confirmed for me on the first day. Now, the Teach for America woman had told us in our five-week summer training what we should do if we didn't have chalkboards. But I had no chalkboards, no paper, pencils, books, no playground. What was hard was the sense that I was supposed to teach with nothing—no experience, no materials.
> Q: *You're quite critical of Teach for America. Why?*
> A: I guess I have a twofold critique. One is that most of the benefit goes to the teachers, not the students. They can parlay their experiences into better careers. Teach for America taps into the feeling of 'I want to do something really good in the world, but I'm not sure what to do.' Well, the organization is well-known and has some status. I think people's intentions are good, but after two years of teaching, you get to move on to what you really want to do. Also, there's enormous need for long-term, not short-term solutions. The teacher shortage is getting worse, not better. I think there are much better models for creating teachers...with real knowledge and experience rather than landing outsiders in communities. If you take a 21 year-old and just place them there, having no awareness of their privilege, not knowing

how to teach, they are not going to do much in that community. They just don't know what the issues are—what's important to the parents, what the community has struggled with. And by the time they might know something; they're burned out and depressed.

Q: *Why is Teach for America so successful in recruiting teachers?*

A: It uses the seductive teacher-as-hero model. On its Web site is a section called 'what it takes' promoting a very individualistic model of the superteacher. The messaging is, 'If you work harder, you'll get your kids on a different track in life.' That's very dangerous because it suggests that if the teachers already there would just work harder, there wouldn't be this achievement gap.

Q: *What did you get out of your experience at Compton?*

A: A whole new understanding of poverty as a kind of violence. The way we set up kids in poor neighborhoods to go to poor schools and do poorly in life, and the violence of that systemic, seemingly intentional policy. I also had to face up to my own privilege. I guess I realized—and this is going to sound very basic—that I got to go to Yale not because I was smart and good but because I was born into a good family that had money. I was able to get the best education that I could buy. I saw that the system was really made for people like me.

Q: *The other teachers weren't very collegial with you. Why?*

A: If I was a veteran teacher in Compton and kept seeing a slew of white women coming in to teach…I don't think I would have been that collegial, either. In my first school, I had some teachers I really liked who were very helpful, but then I was recruited to another Compton school with more problems, a bigger teacher shortage. I looked like another rookie Teach for America teacher—one of eight to 10 white women. Basically, if there's a white teacher in Compton, they're from Teach for America. So the relationships are strained. They see you as an outsider who doesn't know the community and what it takes to become a good teacher.

Q: When did you realize you couldn't stay in Compton?

A: When I went blind in the classroom and couldn't see. I was teaching a math lesson, bending down to work with students, and I started to have blackouts in my eyes—I couldn't see anything. I told the students to see if there was anyone in the yard would could come and get me. A boy stayed with me and held my hand and said not to worry, that help would be on the way. I was eventually taken to the emergency room, where the doctor said that it was either nothing or a brain tumor. Happily, I discovered that it was just a migraine—my migraines started there in Compton. But in that moment, when this wonderful boy was taking care of me and my body was breaking down, I realized that this was not sustainable.

Q: *Tell me about your return visit to Compton last year.*
A: I was trying to track down kids I had taught, which was like trying to track down ghosts. Parents and guardians move a lot, and the children often have different last names. I eventually tracked down three students. One didn't remember me at all, one who didn't seem to be doing well. He was asleep in class when I arrived, and the teacher was having him do a word search on airplanes in English class, which had nothing to do with what he was learning. He said he was really bored in school. He really didn't open up to me. I also felt that things pretty much looked the same in Compton. There was some construction, which was hopeful, and some grass, but as a whole everything was the same. I found it disheartening.
Q: *Did it bother you when the one child couldn't remember you?*
A: No, it put myself in perspective. To me, my experience was a big deal, but to the child it was just 1st grade (Ruenzel 2005).

In 1999 I began my teaching career in Compton also. I was not a part of the Teach for America encroachment, but I saw many of the things Sentilles spoke about. I was not Ivy League, and did not have a stipend provided me on top of my district salary, but I was operating on the same provisional credential they had. These teachers were sought out and guaranteed a job because of the privilege of their educational pedigree, whereas I came searching for employment because LAUSD would only hire me as a substitute teacher with a state university degree. I say this only to show how different the situation was from my perspective. I did not resent the Teach for America teachers. I did, however, witness and overhear the cultural disconnect that Ms. Sentilles talked about. I taught at a continuation high school in Compton Unified, about a block away from the hospital (Martin Luther King Jr.—Drew Medical) that treated her for her attack of blindness. Not to be mean-spirited or vindictive, but it is almost classically tragic that Ms. Sentilles had her vision affected by her time teaching in Compton.

It is a testament to human nature as to how I confirmed that the threat of stereotype operates with equanimity in our society. Having a German-American wife in Wisconsin waiting to re-unite with me while I worked in South Central, one that my colleagues in Compton had no idea about, I heard Black faculty disparage and talk about (in unflattering terms) the White pedagogues in our midst. They spoke to me openly only because they believed, on appearance, that I was expressively authentic to their plight and seeing things through their eyes. Reminiscent, to a large extent of the assuredness that I mentioned the narrator in *The Legend of Sleepy Hollow* talked disparagingly about Blacks. To a great degree I could identify with many of their feelings, but when I heard them talking about Whites in the same way as my wife had heard Whites talking about Blacks when we worked together in a state institution (a reversal of my Compton experience), I knew I couldn't sign a contract for another year there.

Edsource reports that 80% of educators in California are women, and what's more, a majority of them are White. White administrators are overwhelmingly made up of White women also, by some 58%. Teachers are predominately White, with White females also leading statistically in that category with approximately 76%; many of them probably having the same feelings of entitlement that Sarah Sentilles had. The fact is, White women have historically been oriented to fearing, or being wary of, Black males who are approaching their late puberty; it is there whereupon an onset of unease occurs and it can all be rooted back to a 19th century prophecy related to the freeing of slaves, and how society was warned that emancipation would bring about "unnatural" race relations. Thus, miscegenation has been a corporeal plank in the platform for segregation all along; it is seen for some people on both sides of the issue as a race weakening mechanism that produces harm to all parties (Riggs 1987).

Black males have been icons in popular media and oftentimes portrayed as marauding rapists since the filming of *Birth of a Nation*. In that film, spoken of by President Woodrow Wilson as "history writ in lightning" (Riggs 1987), a virginal ingénue commits suicide rather than fall into the hands of a Black pursuer (a White actor in blackface). And unfortunately, the thug and "gangsta" rap styles in music today keeps this very same pathos going. Black male artists in the rap subculture and some females too, scowl and gesticulate with menace in their videos and they make graphic threats of committing rape or murder. This enculturation, to a White educator who has no or little experience with living amongst Blacks, can cause a great deal of anxiety when presented to them. Many Black students repeat the inflammatory lyrics aloud at school, which could cause for a good deal of anxiety to an unprepared audience. Now, it only makes sense that self-preservation is the prime motivation for anyone doing any given thing. Any woman is going to take precautions to prevent her from being assaulted once she concretely imagines that possibility, be it a physical assault, or a verbal altercation.

Looking at someone who just represents that form of menace may be enough to put some teachers at such a level of discomfort that they will go out-of-their-way to have a disciplinary referral at-the-ready, upon the student's arrival. The teacher either hands it to them without explanation, or gives a quick admonishment and an order to leave. Not willing to negotiate in any communication that might keep the child within the classroom because of the perceived threat, the teacher escalates all confrontations that stem from any faux pas in their social index. Raised voices and cultural slights usually ensue and in a theoretical sense, create a sort of Dionysian crisis where every dialogue implies a physical threat, and are reported as being such. And interestingly enough, the Dionysian motif operates within White male educators, as well, because they also tend to react in the same way as their White female counterparts who dislike teaching African American students. Their ploys and rationalizations are extraordinarily the same. The child is always outrageously defiant and has made a threat, or implied a threat. Each time the student returns to the class after being reprimanded the teacher insists they not to return because of some procedural snafu or maybe a document being out of order. When the student argues, both male and female White teachers tend to become shrill and raise their voices. Black males and even more so, Latino males, do not respond well to being yelled at and will more than likely become aggressive. This is unfortunate, but that is an example of the escalation chronology.

Teachers, frankly, teach as they were taught is how the saying goes, but it might be more appropriate to say that teachers teach as they were raised to believe. If both genders of a racially identical group of educators consistently react in the same way to a certain classification of student, there is something systemic operating here. And because of this, at this point, that a slight divergence should be made to expand upon the culture that is the fabric of what White academia in America wraps around its pedagogy. Now, that is not to say that there is segregated pedagogy, per se, but it does imply deference according to majority rule and is what was said before in regards to literature, the semiotic system was set in place there long ago, as well.

Eric Margolis of Arizona State University did a study concerning photography databases of Americana and found that two well-referenced web sites containing pictures of schools and pupils reveal a "hidden curriculum" of misinformation and absence. "To the extent these sites function as important resources for teachers and students searching for primary source documents for history and social study projects, the archives convey significantly biased views of the history of education and minority groups in America " (Margolis 1). This is important, again, due to the connections of perceptions towards making judgments in assessment. Margolis says that the Library of Congress is formatting their approximately 120 million items (photographs) and has at least four million of those available on the World Wide Web. The state of California uses the site as a reference for 35 universities and museums (Margolis 2). With some visual deconstruction it can be seen plainly how a cultural dichotomy had its beginning cemented and furthered through the proliferation of the images in it.

The semiotics given in the visual messages are relative to the value system of American culture and education in the last two centuries. An example of the hidden curriculum can be given by the three pictures, two of them below, taken from the site: These photographs, taken from The Detroit Publishing Company shows White children, lined in front of a monolith of education. In fact, this may be a Catholic school.

The portico frames the orderly ranks and Margolis says it is a metaphor for the "doorway of knowledge," something dark and intimidating, something much higher than the individual who must pass through it. Yet, these children are allowed to pass through the entrance and stand surrounded by the entry; their white clothing imbues them with symbolizations of innocence and purity. The photographs are not captioned with any indication as to their subjects' ethnicity, and some would say it's probably due to the fact that it is all too apparent that the children are White. Margolis says that "white" is the norm; it is the given; it is understood. Where no race is specified, or even connoted, one assumes Whiteness. Any references for pictures on the site for "white students" or "white teachers" have no links. "'Whites' are only identified as such in opposition to people of color, whereas people of color always have their ethnicity attached as a marker and identifier" (10). The defense I provided for the absence of the indicator was that it is apparent the class members are White. Well, the photo below on the left is just as transparent, yet the caption for it is "Four black children in yard", and which, by the way, was a photograph taken along the same time, and owned by the very same company that took the other one of the White children at the city school.. The photo on the right is called "Negro children standing in front of half mile fence…" This was taken in Detroit in 1942, and the wall in it separates a Black neighborhood from a White residential area:

Margolis says that the image collection of the Detroit Photographic Company had 300 school photographs when he used it, but not a one showed anyone other than White students in school. Enlarging his search for "Black Children" broadened the base to 25,000 photos, but still only six items were in the collection's total (Margolis 11). To be fair, however, there has been a good deal of additions to the collection since Margolis perused the database. When I did my research I found a quantity of photographs with African American child subjects in them, and not all of them were depictions of stereotypical pickanninies. And there were also pictures identifying subjects as "White". Yet, there was a disturbing pre-school book, circa 1928, of "Little Black Sambo" that I found incredible to see listed; as well, and cover music and lyrics for a song called, "Little Black One Like Me". Written by a Jewish author, the song is voiced from the perspective of an African American child, inquiring if there were angels in heaven who were black. What are the subliminal differences between the four photographs on the last two pages? For one, the photographer did not have the African American children get dressed up, though they might have had nicer clothes.

Margolis says that the reason the children are depicted this way is to solidify the notion to white consumers that black children would rather be out in fields rather than in school (11). They would not be shown in images portraying cleanliness, neatness and order, and definitely not looking innocent and virtuous. That could be self-serving on Margolis's part, though. I found pictures of Black students, who didn't attend school until after January 1st, and cotton-picking was over, and I found pictures of White students in Kentucky who didn't go when "syrupping" was being conducted. Regardless, the pictures shown are what is called, according to P.A. Turner a 'contemptible collectible,' postcards produced for white consumers that graphically represented race stereotypes. This database, however slanted, is still one that is linked to institutions of higher learning today, and does have a group of collections called "The African American Odyssey," but that is separate from the "American Memory" grouping, and furthermore, that particular group does not have access to any photographs being in it, even still today.

Although, it might possibly be that the images are inaccessible because they have not yet been digitized, it still makes one wonder why the Webmaster didn't balance what pictures were being formatted to show on the site? This frames the overall problem I have presented thus far. It shows how the widespread the scope of marginalization is in our country. That marginalization has come to be such an adverse affect to our society that it eventually came to jeopardize the validity of most high stakes writing assessments, in general, and for African Americans it is specifically deleterious. It can make capital gains for the purveyor and at the same time funnel hatred from ideologues towards Blacks if socioeconomic environments destabilize, as is seemingly ratified by the student comments about Blacks causing the school's testing malaise. And as I stated earlier, the seeds of doubt about Black student achievement is planted quite early.

My own grandson, an effervescent, precocious, five year-old is being considered to be held back in kindergarten for another year, when at this time his grades have him at a high "C" to a low "B" level. The first CSTs for him won't be given until he is in the 3rd grade. He is the only African American child in his class. Yet, historically, as the visual record shows, even though there may possibly have been pockets of hope in regards to early signs of integration, as shown below, perceptions have always placed limits:

The picture above, on the left, is from the Schomburg Collection from the New York Public Library, and it is a site that Margolis says has better catalogs in reference to African American student representation. It is picture of a class in 1912 Pennsylvania, and its caption is 'Class of school children posing outside with their teacher'. The teacher appears to be White but Margolis says she is actually Black, and that they might all be grouped together because the White classmates may be immigrants, and just as much an "other" as the non-whites (13.) The flip side of the coin could also be that these students were of mixed blood. To the right, is a picture taken in 1932, in Georgia. These siblings were from a mixed relationship, one parent being white, and the other half-black (mulatto *sic*), or quarter black (octoroon *sic*).

These children refused to take pictures with African American peers, and yet they could not find acceptance amongst whites, either. They are photographic proof of how easily the scenario of "passing for white" could be undertaken by those so inclined. What might also give some cultural validity to Margolis' supposition about "otherness" is that Pennsylvania is predominately conservative and non-indulgent. In fact, even today, a well-known Democratic political strategist, James Carville, restated once on an NBC *Meet the Press* segment an old saying about the state; a feeling that the culture there may be more conducive to a White woman winning the state's primary rather than an African American male, although neither minority has ever been elected to high office there. "Pennsylvania is Philadelphia on one end," Carville said, "and Pittsburg on the other, with Alabama in between" (3/23/08). And Carville also made it clear that he was not talking about Black Alabama. It is quite likely that things weren't any better in that part of the country practically a hundred years ago than they are today. It is also quite likely that Carville's analysis is on point with the zeitgeist across the whole country, especially in places removed from diverse cities. It is there where the persona of African Americans cannot be scrutinized accurately because of their absence in the demographics and then the tainted ethnic notions of African American capability can come in to fill that void.

This conversation about the dichotomy between these two races of haves and have-nots can be summed up in the above photographs. They are both from schools in Georgia, one for Whites, and one for Blacks. And as in the Pennsylvania photograph, the teacher in the doorway is a lightly complected African American woman, not a White one. These pictures are almost of a vintage that they would be public domain items, if they weren't already government photos, but even today we have similar disparity in schools that have affluence and those that don't. But it is not only images that polarize some White Americans about their uneasy proximity to Black Americans.

"Race is about how you use your language," Michael Eric Dyson writes in his new book *April 4, 1968: Martin Luther King Jr's Death. And How it Changed America Forever* (229). Now, I have connected that statement to my thesis by referring to, and deconstructing, the language that has been used to write about African Americans (beginning with Washington Irving); the convention of language and dialect used in popular contrivances (minstrel ideology and in modern media), and lastly how African Americans speak about themselves to one another, and to the world at large.

CHAPTER FIVE
The Ebonics Debate

When one considers the velocity of the double-coding that's capable between their forays into Black and White language paradigms, and how easily it's done, it can be argued that African Americans are actually more bilingual than they realize. Yet, then why are there not more African Americans mainstreamed? Replicating exact syntax and writing conventions and mechanisms have always been attainable for African Americans, and in the past they were striven for, something to be mastered, but many today, I have found, will not even bother with learning such skills of elocution. They do not shift vernaculars when it is prudent to do so. And they will not adhere to tense markers, sometimes even in formal settings. They just seem content on segregating themselves through racial isolation of their own choosing. These African Americans purely realize that their very essence can be unpleasant to certain members of the White race; so, they therefore refrain from switching to the culture of power's language code when in the presence of Anglo Americans. After all, the perception that African Americans are culturally inferior has existed ever since the beginning of popular culture in the colonies; it is engrained like a tap root into the American fabric. For the non-comporting African Americans, their single code of communication that is adhered to so strongly, is perhaps held on to so assiduously because it is so identifiable to them with who they believe they are, essentially. While popular culture has always portrayed the African American as unappealing, unless designated as a subordinate, being erudite to Whites is then not only expected of authentic African Americans, but is demanded of them by their peers. The non-assimilated African American, therefore, celebrates in anything and everything that reinforces their Black heritage because Anglo heritage, up to this point, has not.

What is antithetical to that culture is the dialect of Black English. AAVE has linguistic markers, such as the incorrect use of idiomatic expressions and two-word verb forms, that are clearly seen as being non-standard, that leaves evaluators so hung up on the poor mechanics employed by some of their Black students that they seem to overlook any positives in the writing that the work contains. They discount the fact that it may have the potential (e.g. race neutral potential) to becoming more fully formed; if given time and guidance, things that they are not willing to provide, the positives are simply glossed over in the evaluator's judgment. Said positives can be given to you as an example drawn from the real experience of a non-traditional student who is African American (Harley, 1996).

Though this anecdote pertains to an entry-level experience, it still seems to show the same possibility of the "threat of stereotype" being a cause-and-effect factor in her poor assessment, as it reflects the experience of many others.

Kay Harley and Sally I. Cannon discuss a female by the name of Mica who attended Saginaw Valley State University in Michigan (1996). This woman was taking a class in Basic English, having passed the placement assessment to get her into a core curriculum class. The instructor was doing exactly what CCCC wants teachers to do; he was being multifaceted in making written assessments of students through a progression of assignments in their curriculum. He was allowing assessment to be based on a variety of work over a period of time. He had assignments containing pre-writing essays and post-impromptu essays. He had a multiple-choice test for covering the concepts of mechanics and grammar. This then, should have ensured, and allowed enough time for Mica making adjustments, or to "reinforce good teaching" and thereby gaining improvement in her performance (Harley 75). Yet, in the end analysis she failed her final, which was a portfolio. She evidently had insufficient criteria used against her all along, and the authors believe that the expectations of the instructor distorted the way he looked at any composition with identified non-standard structure and mechanics.

That is in opposition to the inclusiveness of the CCCC policy statement. The authors noted in their analysis of the woman's work that she demonstrated a "strong emotive voice", and that she was "confident in her use of personal anecdotes." They felt her work had elements in it that were acceptable and proper for the assignment. The writers therefore advise that there be an extended effort to recognize the current theory about non-standard vernacular, in order to give credit its rightful recognition and also realizing that change can only be effected through gaining knowledge. Similar tendencies have also been reported by black graduate students of English at CUNY (Bruna). Their insights were transcribed from an on-line discussion in 1998 and they say that it was their experience to witness the assessment system at the school to be "philosophically bankrupt", blind as to what they should look for when making equitable assessments. They talk about how composition classes tended to be a composition instructor "cheerleading for assimilation" between non-standard to standard language usage; they also talked about how reading—followed by writing interpretively about what you just read, did not occur. Reading and writing were divided subjects in their curriculum and not conjoined for reciprocal learning. They were silenced.

These students did what many African Americans have done over the decades; they used the ability to code-switch at the appropriate place and the appropriate time to compensate for their lack of a platform to be expressive. They followed the norm in order to succeed, and that required them not to refer to their culture by writing in a way that would resemble something identifiably African American. This threat of stereotype caused anxiety enough for the six of them to commiserate over it (Bruna 73-95). This goes to show then, that indeed the practices alluded to in this book do seem to be experienced by a significant number of African American students, and other students of color, across the span of education. It even corroborates some of the feelings expressed to me on campus.

In addition, they recognize many mainstream academic writers are using some of the same rhetoric and style in their writing but as Helmers pointed out, there is a mentality of do as I say, not as I do, when it comes to scholarly writing, for the most part. And even with this case study and others being done to research the issue, the NCTE and CCCC still have no real jurisdictional power over educators. They can only recommend to legislators, school boards, and districts what action should be taken to improve the situation for Blacks and other non-white students. The implementation of the policy is in the hands of the local stakeholders in the schools and colleges. And they can take it as far as they want, or choose to ignore it altogether. Notwithstanding its association with these watchdog organizations and their standards, the policies are no more than curriculum guidelines to the educational institutions, and are not consigning to them.

What is this language comprised of that signals such a cogent meaning amongst many White teachers and intellects (and some Blacks, as well) that there should be a relegation to some lower perception anything attributive to a person using non-standard vernacular? This goes aside of the structuralist medium that images convey to meaning, and it actually goes into what makes up that meaning, itself. Unfortunately, the linguistics applied to Ebonics and its debate also help to support the iconic images that already make up stereotypes about African Americans.

Spoken language and class are more intertwined than race and class, it seems, because it can be truly argued that some White Appalachians or White West Virginians have dialects that connote them also being uneducated people, and just as susceptible to stereotype as African Americans. With that being said, however, they can also "clean up" quite well, and if educated will have more privilege than an African American with the same education. The skin color of the "poor trash" has not been held to be bankrupt; it is only the falling short of their potential that keeps them outside. But even they, in their limited capacity, are held higher socially than African Americans, on the whole.

In regards to the Standard English vs. non-standard English debate, Betsy Winsboro wants there to be an exchange to occur between those who speak

Black English and the educators who make the curriculum operate, and that reciprocal transfer could include materials that create inclusive opportunities in learning:

> Studies consistently demonstrate that educators manifest a generally negative reaction to the "less familiar dialect" in favor of Standard English. Black educators themselves have long recognized the possible socioeconomic disadvantages of speaking a black dialect in a predominantly white society. There is empirically based evidence of teacher bias against black students, and it is obvious that listeners may not limit their criteria for judgment strictly to quantifiable data. Furthermore, if students are labeled as less capable and are then treated as such, they will probably begin to display characteristics of those who indeed are less capable of speaking and writing formal English (18).

For cultural reasons, Winsboro stresses, it is important that non-standard dialect not be eradicated, but she offers no other benefit of using the language other than it is seen by some to be a reifying, positive self-portrayal. She stresses education about non-standard dialect and tolerance. On the other hand, she also matter-of-factly claims that the sign of success today is really having the ability to be upwardly mobile, to be in demand. Once the speakers of Black English completes acquiring and utilizing the skills in communication that the culture of power values, they will be a commodity who can then earn good money for their labor, whereas before it was taken free gratis from them through forced servitude. And while it is truly valued, and can transcend the individual, the requirements of the assimilation can also whip them into submission.

Case in point is the situation that happened to a middle-aged African American woman (who had been participating in foster care for decades) who had two of her foster children (African American males of about nine and eleven years) taken away from her by the New York Child Protection Services (*Dateline* 2004). The reason for the extraction wasn't because of physical abuse, or neglect. The reason the boys were being taken from their foster care parent was that they had been identified with a learning disability, and it was believed that the foster home they were in would damage their chances of battling their disabilities because "Lisa" spoke nonstandard English. In fact, she was a descendant of the Gullah island people off the Carolinas, and she regularly used the vernacular accustomed to her own upbringing. The New York family courts felt that, in effect, a parent not having mastered Standard English is not equipped to be able to reinforce and support the language skill modifications and strategies the children needed to have modeled. To be exact, the courts said she herself had a learning disability.

Lisa admitted that at times she talked rapidly, and that her words might run together into a seemingly unintelligible gibberish, but that is actually what

Kenneth Pike describes happening to many in his language wave, particle, and field theories (Covino 593). Lines of sound distinction (word boundaries) are broken down through informal context and lackadaisical performance: either through lack of energy, necessity of communicative urgency, or cultural identification in the vernacular lexicon between the speaker and their audience. The point is, everyone does this in fact, whether they are speaking nonstandard or Standard English. The courts were arguing, however, that the ADA disability rights of the children, to have a "least restrictive environment," had to extend to the home because the court had the ultimate jurisdiction and responsibility over the children. It placed them in the home of a caretaker, and had to assure that the boys would not be neglected in regards to the behavior modifications needed to allay their learning disabilities.

Coming to her defense was the New York University School of Law at the behest of Lisa's former foster child. This young man, who was a student in the law school and who happens to be Anglo American, had a learning disability during all his years with Lisa, and nonetheless became an attorney in Pennsylvania. Linguists and other specialists were hired by the law school to build a defense for Lisa, and her former child worked long hours doing legal research on her behalf. He was not willing to let the legal precedent be set in America that a vernacular employed by an individual could be used against them to deny consortium with family members. After practically two years, Lisa has been reunited with the boys and she formally adopted them. This definitely makes a strong statement that linguistics can indeed have a salient interdependency in an individual's life, but it also speaks as to whether learning Standard English is now being demanded by our culture. Is this propensity an elitist position or a commonsensical viewpoint borne out necessity?

Four years ago, while first taking methodology courses to gain a teaching credential, I wrote a position paper on a professional article that I found slightly disturbing at that time. Abha Gupta's "What's up wif Ebonics, Ya'll?" seemed to rub against the little goodwill I had about nonstandard English and its speakers. Being African American, and able to remember sitting in segregated theater seats with my grandfather, I had problems with anyone's approval for using the dialect. I knew how anything that exacerbated, by signification, my all too apparent complexion was the antithesis of what I desired. For one, the vernacular denoted a lower-scale lifestyle than I wanted attributed to me; it also made for a point of ridicule by the majority culture of Standard English speakers around me, and it also failed in being able to produce truly aesthetic communication. In fact, it was my belief that Ebonics, or African American Vernacular English (AAVE), or Inner City English (ICE), or Black Vernacular English (BVE), whatever term you wanted to call it, could only be synthesized into minimal surface structures, and no abstract concept, say appropriate for a thesis statement, could ever come of it. To further aggravate me, Gupta wished that pedagogues and scholars would use the dialect in the prose of *The Adventures of Huckleberry Finn* to illustrate the linguistic systems in the language form. To me, that was outside the realm of reason, for that novel used stereotype and bigoted epithets liberally within its boundaries and I, for one, refused to teach it for literature in my high school, as was my right and choice.

Gupta quotes K. Au, who says, "Multiethnic literature can be used to affirm the cultural identity of students of diverse backgrounds and to develop all students' understanding and appreciation of other cultures (176)." Gupta extends Au's idea by informing the reader that differences in language forms are best demonstrated in the realistic literature of particular authors:

> For example, in *Huckleberry Finn*, Mark Twain shows how social belief systems of communities can be based on language use. Such literature can be read aloud and discussed to make students aware of different genres, techniques of creating dialogue and using language for a purpose, and writing for a particular audience.

The issue to be taken with using *Huckleberry Finn*, however, as a model for the use of different language forms, goes beyond the fact that it is realist satire that maligns a collective group of people with caricature and stereotype (e.g. the word *nigger* being used over three hundred times). Reading *Huck Finn* will simply not accomplish the dialect creation of awareness in the student that Gupta alludes to have sought. Gupta expects an expressivity, a learning experience for the students taking place where they can learn all they need to know about how they, themselves, acquire and utilize different language forms, from simply reading and responding to this book, and others like it. In turn, Gupta proposes, that this can hopefully enable students to have an objective viewpoint as to how society affects the reading of a text. This is a noble idea, but it disintegrates in its implementation. Kathleen McCormick examined what really happens with using *Huck Finn*, for just such a purpose, in her book *The Culture of Reading and the Teaching of English*.

McCormick said that two teachers in the South were using the text to "develop within students a sense of their own and the text's social construction." This would relate to expression of the students' historical and cultural experiences regarding such subject matter such as: "Klu Klux Klan episodes ...as recently as 1986, clashes between two working class groups," and it would also allow for the students to find their own voice in the discourse. There was also the use of pre-writing materials (journals) that went through three proposed phases of objectification: first, focusing on the student, secondly, training attention on the text, and then finally extending the thinking to larger themes:

> While the lesson is supposedly that one's beliefs are socially constructed, White and 'Pritchard do not acknowledge the extent to which the classroom situation itself might be constructing their students' responses. They simply fall back on a naive expressivism; "We encourage them to maintain their personal voices and write honest, expressive responses"...nor do they carry this gesture towards social

construction through to their students' reading of the text of *Huckleberry Finn*. For if students are, at least in part, constructed by their environment, *Huckleberry Finn*, which is institutionally part of that environment, must also be working to construct them in particular ways which they will presumably...accept or resist. But the text is not presented to them in this way (McCormick 43).

An African American student didn't have a problem with the text because its author wasn't alive, anyway, and didn't present an immediate threat: "Even if Mark Twain was being prejudiced what difference would it make now the man is dead. It couldn't have bothered people back in those days because most slaves didn't know any better (McCormick 44)." The student could not see that differences in a text reading could occur depending from what place in history the text is being presented; he or she also could not realize how prejudice could be considered harmful within any time period. The southern teachers did not go beyond studying the text of *Huck Finn*, as a whole, and the subjective analysis of the book's characters, in disregard of their third objective for the unit. Students were not aware of how to make metacognitive associations to the larger issues of the social dynamics used in vernaculars. This happened through the failure of the pedagogues not explicitly pointing out such differences in the text and guiding the connections to be made. Notwithstanding the textual implications of accepting and studying nonstandard English in a critical sense, the issue of pragmatics seems to be an overriding concern needing further deliberation. Nonstandard English denotes a class of people, and therefore identity is at issue here and should be discussed.

Using the concept of cultural identity developed by Hegel (a person's identity is defined by everything that they are not) called "determinate negation," events, trends, and patterns in literary and linguistic structure and semiotics are products of striving for a "code" that represents who people are within a culture. Houston A. Baker Jr. believes that African American "vernacular" holds the tendrils to these elements, and must be further defined in order to understand this race of people. According to the editors of *The Norton Anthology of Literary Theory and Criticism*, the word vernacular, itself, is derived from the "special Latin vocabulary of slavery." Literally, it describes a slave who is not bought by the master, but born into the master's estate. Linguistically, it refers to a nonstandard language or dialect in a region. Baker holds that to study vernacular is "to study how a particular language is used by just those speakers who have not been in the social position to use or create the 'standard' language."

> How do those whose speech carries no authority and who are usually expected to be silent use the master's language differently than the master himself does? How do they make that language, so often employed to oppress them, serve their own purposes and needs: What

resources are to be found within those 'nonstandard dialects' created by speakers far form the centers of power? (Leitch 2225).

One troubling and identifiable subordination of Standard English to a vernacular is in the reversal that has been applied to the racist term, *nigger*, which is, as was mentioned earlier, used contextually about 300 times in *The Adventures of Huckleberry Finn*. Many African Americans, for decades, have taken that term being applied to them (originally by the former masters and descendants who owned slaves) and metamorphosed the moniker into a cultural positive. The term *nigga*, or *niggah* in modern day use, is signifying an African American who is true to their self-assessed culture, and one who is unafraid and unapologetic for being aggressively assertive about that identity. Whites cannot use the word casually amongst African Americans, despite there being a mutual understanding between them that a new meaning is being implied. Due to the oppressive legacy of Whites referring to Blacks as "niggers" in the past, even a derivation of it being uttered is anathema. According to Randall Kennedy, saying the word can be a mitigating defense in a physical assault by an African American upon a White (54). I doubt, however, that this is the kind of usurpation that Baker had in mind when he asked his former question about how Blacks can use a language reversal to enrich and empower.

There are probably a myriad of words and phrases that theoretically could be reconstructed regarding African Americans that could become positive attributes, but that word is not one of them. Despite the legal aegis given to African Americans over hate significations, the response to the nonstandard word being used by Anglo Americans almost ratifies how racists would say African Americans are subhuman. To the African American youth of today, those who are enamored with using the assignation over and over again in referring to anyone who is African American be they young or old, the words of Malcolm X might prove enlightening. Not only did he object to the use of the word, he also explained his distaste over an acceptance of being called "negroes", as well. In a speech on Afro-American Unity that was to be given on the day of his assassination, though not the speech meant for the Audubon, Malcolm X wrote:

> Another term, 'negro' is erroneously used and is degrading in the eyes of informed and self-respecting persons of African heritage. It denotes stereotyped and debased traits of character and classifies a whole segment of humanity on the basis of false information. From all intelligent viewpoints, it is a badge of slavery and helps to prolong and perpetuate oppression and discrimination. Persons who recognize the emotional thrust and plain show of disrespect in the southerner's use of 'nigra' and the general use of 'nigger' must also realize that all three words are essentially the same. The other two: 'nigra' and 'nigger' are blunt and undeceptive. The one representing respectability, 'negro,' is merely the same substance in a polished package and spelled with a

capital letter. This refinement is added so that a degrading terminology can be legitimately used in general literature and 'polite' conversation without embarrassment (Clark 265).

When I was born, in the late 50's my birth certificate declared that I was "colored". By the time I entered kindergarten and was guaranteed that I'd have the right to vote 12 years later, Negro was the pejorative I was referred to by our society; and although I came to believe it was a step up from the former category, within four years I found that "Black" was the new nominative; actually, one could choose being called either Black or Afro-American. Now, it's African American or Black being used, possibly because afros were more analogous to a hairstyle worn at one time by both Black and White Americans, and therefore being less distinct as to race, but more indicative of culture. Afro Asian could also be lumped in with Afro American nomenclature. After studying more of Malcolm X, however, I now understand why many latter day Black students I encounter become offended by being referred to as a Negro. But what I cannot fathom is how being identified as "nigga" is somehow a better attribute. Malcolm considered one to be as bad as the other, for the simple fact that the words have similar linguistic origins:

> The term 'negro' developed from a word in the Spanish language which is actually an adjective (describing word) meaning 'black,' that is, the *color* black. In plain English, if someone said or was called a 'black' or a 'dark,' even a young child would very naturally question. 'A black what?' or 'A dark what?' because adjectives do not name, they describe. Please take note that in order to make use of this mechanism, a word was transferred from another language and deceptively changed in function from an adjective to a noun, which is a naming word. Its application in the nominative (naming) sense was intentionally used to portray the article as being 'all alike and all the same.' It denotes: a 'darkie,' a slave, a subhuman, an ex-slave, a *'negro.'* Afro-Americans must reanalyze and particularly question our own use of this term, keeping in mind all the facts. In light of the historical meanings and current implications, all intelligent and informed Afro-Americans and Africans continue to reject its use in the noun form as a proper adjective. Its usage shall continue to be considered as unenlightened and objectionable or deliberately offensive whether in speech or writing. We accept the use of Afro-American, African, and Black man in reference to persons of African heritage. To every other part of mankind goes this measure of just respect. We do not desire more nor shall we accept less (Clark 266).

Malcolm X would often deride his contemporary, Dr. Martin Luther King, Jr. for referring to Blacks as Negroes. Growing up, I remember my family being raised to follow the non-confrontational King precept, and identified myself as a Negro. My cousins who lived 65 miles north, in Chicago, however, liked to use the Afrocentric nominatives. Hearing Dr. King say the word was different than when I would hear John F. Kennedy or Robert F. Kennedy use it. Amongst Blacks, we said Negro with a shortened vowel in the first syllable; however, all enlightened Whites using the term always elongated the vowel, "Nee-grow". I remember, even at a very young age, that the word was uncomfortable for me to hear; for even with the deliberate care not to be mistaken for having said it, hearing "Nee-grow" spoken by a White person had the same meaning and conveyance to me as hearing them say nigger. To me it seemed a linguistic backstabbing. Henry Louis Gates Jr., a centrist African American literary theorist and historian, wrote that In the 19th Century, Alexander Crummell, who fomented language acquisition in Liberia for many years of his life, devoted his energies to dispelling "the denial of intellectuality in the Negro; the assertion that he was not a human being" (Leitch 2425).

As a teenager, Crummell recounted an incident he overheard between a South Carolina senator and a lawyer at an Anti-slavery office in New York City. John C. Calhoun, the senator, was overheard to say that if he ever found a Negro who could master Greek syntax, he would believe in Negro humanity and treat the Negro as a man. This inspired Crummell to go to England and learn the Greek language at Cambridge. Later, he decided it was not so much the language that separated the races, but the exclusion of the Negro from the Western Culture. In 1860 he said, "In the English language are embodied 'the noblest theories of liberty' and 'the grandest ideas of humanity.' If black people master the master's tongue, these great and grand ideas will become African ideas, because 'ideas conserve men, and keep alive the vitality of nations. " Crummell believed African vernacular and "neo-African" vernacular should be abandoned. He said, "All low, inferior, and barbarous tongues are, doubtless, but the lees and dregs of noble languages, which have gradually, as the soul of a nation has died out, sunk down to degradation and ruin. We must not suffer this decay on these shores, in this nation." Gates, however, later refutes Crummell, and echoes Houston Baker's Hegelian ideology that Black language can only exist within the context as to what is different from it in the master narrative. "We as critics must turn to our own peculiarly black structures of thought and feeling to develop our own languages of criticism. We must do so by drawing on the black vernacular, the language we use to speak to each other when no outsiders are around." If Black culture obfuscates itself by taking to heart the master narrative in White criticism, Gates believes, the African American will "sink…remain alienated …masked…singing… reflecting our bald heads":

> We must redefine theory itself from within our own black cultures, refusing to grant the racist premise that theory is something that white people do, so that we are doomed to imitate our white colleagues, like reverse black minstrel critics done up in whiteface. We are all heirs to critical theory, but critics are also heir to the black vernacular crit-

ical tradition as well. We must not succumb, as did Alexander Crummell, to the tragic lure of white power, the mistake of accepting the empowering language of white critical theory as universal or as our only language, the mistake of confusing the enabling mask of theory with our own black faces...we must at last don the empowering mask of blackness and talk that talk...While it is true that we must, as Du Bois said...'know and test the power of the cabalistic letters of the white man,' we must know and test the dark secrets of a black discursive universe that awaits its disclosure through the black arts of interpretation (Leitch 2432).

The following derivatives, from various sources, make up the consistent rules associated with nonstandard English usage. Repetitive studies have confirmed beyond a doubt that AAVE [African American Vernacular English] has the characteristics of any language; it is considered as rule-governed and as logical as SAE. In addition, there are salient and high-ordered relationships between nonstandard and standard English. The common aspects of the dialect are:

1. Present tense forms of the verb 'to be' are often dropped in casual speech: *She* [is] *the first one* [who] *started us off*.
2. ICE (Inner-City English) has the option of deleting a contractible form of 'to be': *They* [are] *not caught*.
3. The verb *to be* (as well as other auxiliary verbs) becomes reduced in casual speech when it is unstressed [and] happens quite generally in the informal style in all dialects of American English.
4. [In relation to ICE] the *to be* verb has been termed *invariant be* (since it does not vary either to reflect past or present tense, or to agree with the subject)...it indicates a habitual and repeatable action, state, or event...typically used in general descriptions...and to indicate customary or typical states of affairs: *My father* [is usually] *'be' the last one to open his presents*.

The verb *to be*, in ICE, is not invariant, however, when a relationship shows permanence or is in the present tense, therefore, "the sentence: *You* [are] *makin' sense, but you don't* [usually] *be makin' sense*...suggests that one could...mean: 'That's a bright remark—but it's not the usual thing for you.' The use of invariant *be* has been cited as a grammatical feature unique to ICE, representing what seems to be a genuine difference between ICE and other American English dialects (Arkmajian 294).

I believe, however, as thorough as Michael Linn and Linda Miller-Cleary were in describing NSAE, they didn't quite go far enough with explaining one of their rules for AAVE. But it is the most salient of the markers of the dialect. Linn and Miller-Cleary state in structure rule #2 that the *to be* verb can either be contracted or not, in AAVE. Anyone I've ever heard use Ebonics, however, has never used a standard contracted verb when they're talking unless it is with the invariant *to be* sense after a primary verbal phrase drops the invariant. They would say the Linn's sentence: *You* [are] *makin' sense, but you don't* [usually] *be makin' sense* and perform it in this way: *You* [are] *makin' sense, but you ain't* [usually] *makin' sense*. Or it could be said like this: *You be* [are] *makin' sense, but you don't* [usually] *be makin' sense*. A double invariant *to be* phrasal is used: "You be—you don't be". All tense markers are either completely eradicated or doubled and they are saying: you aren't making sense at all times, in the present, and will invariably not make much sense in any other time in the future. And I've never seen a user of Ebonics use a Standard English contraction in their writing. This rule then that Linn and Miller-Cleary declare may occur in various regions of the country that I'm not aware of, but I've as yet to see it demonstrated in my life and experience as an African American.

Other tendencies noted by linguists are a similarity between AAVE and Chinese American dialects: both avoiding *double signification in plurals* (e.g. "two dog") and a relation to an Early American use of a *repeated subject* ('The boy, he...as in 'Thy rod and thy staff, they...') and the *reinforced negative* ('Nobody don't...'), commonplace in Shakespeare's plays (Newman 279). Even more confusing is that some researchers may be talking about the same thing, but for the sake of publishing autonomy coin a term of their own; case in point, Linn's reclassification for a form of *invariant be*:

> Differences between varieties may be either qualitative or quantitative in nature. In qualitative differences, linguistic forms found in one variety are categorically absent in another variety...the use of so-called 'distributive be' ...as a characteristic of Vernacular Black variety is a structure which is completely absent from the systems of many other varieties of English. Hence, we may speak of *'distributive* be' as a form which demonstrates qualitative differences among the varieties of English (119).

It's strange to me that all these linguists don't all list the same rule structures as being common in Ebonics. They seem to have basic agreements about the vernacular but differ on how they present their sentiments on the subject, using nuance to particularize their theory. The one variant that runs within each text, however, is that they all claim information pertaining about the *to be* verb usage as being the significant marker of the dialect. And this is all well and good, and the prerogative of a scholar, but the pragmatic approach to this theory is how the subject feels about the analysis.

My sentiment was more or less like that of Farrell, Hirsch, and others, that practitioners of nonstandard English were qualifiedly, if not quantitatively, deficient in the language processes needed for success in school. I fought connotative Ebonics chains throughout most my life, and now, as a mature adult, couldn't tolerate I was being told I should embrace its hybrid legacy. Gupta's premise for her article was the maxim, "a child's language is not a problem to be fixed but is a resource for learning". She inferred that just as students have different modalities in learning concepts, they should also be expected to communicate in various forms of expression, and that teachers should allow for this in their assessments. I used to believe that this was counter-productive.

With four years of graduate study, however, I've somewhat softened my thinking in regards to learning Ebonics, because I now understand the need for the dialect better. That does not mean I comprehend it any better, or the passion for its extemporaneous use, but I just am not as virulent in my disdain for people using it around me, narrow-minded as that may seem. I've come to accept the fact that there are psychosocial factors at work in my mindset, and not just matters of personal preference that cause me to embrace SAE. Michael Linn and Linda Miller-Cleary emphasize the following in their book, *Linguistics for Teachers*, when discussing how African Americans have variable expressions of nonstandard styling within their dialects:

> The dimension of style appears to differ in its significance at various periods in the life cycle of an individual, although it is present to some extent at all periods…reduced stylistic variation in the earliest stages is due to the acquisitional process…sensitivity to the social significance of various styles usually precedes a full stylistic repertoire. During the later periods of life, adults have typically resigned themselves to their particular status and role in American society…this is manifested in language by the reduction in the range of stylistic fluctuation…intermediate social classes, such as the lower middle class, may be expected to show more stylistic variation than the upper middle class (118).

During my acquisition phase I was not around people who used nonstandard English, and when I did become aware of it and its styling, I used it sparingly and informally. I grew up in a small Midwestern town that had maybe nine hundred African Americans in it. I rarely, if ever, would utilize this speech when around Whites. Coming from a lower middle class background, I always desired to improve my station in life. When Linn and Miller-Cleary say that there may be more stylistic variation from my former status, it is difficult to say whether they mean there are more distinct differences in the dialect of someone of the lower class, or that the lower class is more apt to switch back and forth between standard and nonstandard English. Whatever the explanation, there are exceptions to every rule, as the saying goes, and I beg to differ with the authors. In my case, it was not only materialism that motivated my speech choices, but the desire for self-improvement, a state of mind with an ideal behind it. I was clearly lower middle class, but spoke in the manner of someone from the upper middle class because I imagined myself as that.

Steven and Susan Tchudi examine how teachers react to and administer strategies for encounters with students who use nonstandard dialects. They seem to be politically correct in the way they make judgments about the students, but there are points where they have some racist tinge to their commentaries. Going over the history of teaching English in America they say teachers taught Standard English as a status dialect, "It is a 'prestige' or standard dialect more as a result of the power of its speakers...than any innate superiority or elegance" (211). Though being forthright in admitting that all dialects are pragmatic, as far as being able to communicate ideas, they contradict themselves as to how acceptable they perceive those who utilize nonstandard dialects are:

> Kids who don't use standard spellings will have their job applications rejected; those who employ nonstandard usage in placement tests will wind up in remedial writing courses (even though they may be quite articulate). Folks who write in standard English have a better chance of having their letters to the editor published; those who speak SE will be listened to more carefully in public settings than those who don't (if the latter can even work up the needed moxie to speak publicly in the first place) (211).

Within one fell swoop the Tchudis allude to nonstandard speakers having the demonstrated ability to be effervescent in their speech, and then smugly comment that nonstandard speakers probably would be reticent to speak in a formal situation. People who use nonstandard dialects are generally anything but shy, as Zora Neale Hurston memorably stated. They might not come up with the most logical discourse, and it will not have the elocutionary wherewithal of a preferred speaker, but they can and will speak their minds without provocation. The Tchudis are being condescending here in a troubling way. While I may not care to be around people who use nonstandard English consistently, it doesn't take away other personal attributes that can outweigh their social faux pas in speaking. I would not cast dispersions about these people. They are part of my essence and should not be ridiculed in that way.

> We of course recognize that Standard English 'matters,' that there are penalties for the inability to use it in certain situations. We also state unequivocally that correctness matters, that the schools have a responsibility to prepare students who can write for a variety of audiences, including putting the finishing touches on surface structure (213).

Teachers are categorized by the Tchudis under three different categories of pedagogical styles in relation to how they approach the teaching of Standard English in their classes. They are either *enforcers*: accepting only the standard dialect; bidialectilists: who guide students to standard usage while not discriminating against their natural dialects; or they are *expansionists*: advocating a homogenous understanding of language by expanding opportunities to use language in intertextual ways.

Of the three, it's readily understood that the enforcer position is the least accepted in teaching methods, but old habits die-hard. This "old school" stance still pervades many of the teaching schemas of credential students. Bidialectic methodology would seem tolerant enough, but the Tchudis point out that this approach still points in only one direction to accomplish change. The Anglo American students do not have to gain any understanding of the nonstandard dialect; it is the minority speakers who must always adjust. Still there are others who feel bidialecticism is the way to go. Beth Newman is of the opinion that bidialectism is the proper method, contrary to what the Tchudis maintain:

> Knowledge is empowering; ignorance is limiting. By helping our students [through dialectism] to fluency in the standard dialect, we empower them to join the established system if that is their desire or, should they choose to oppose the established system, such fluency empowers them to oppose it on far better terms (283).

It is the summation of that quote's first sentence that reverberates within academics and criticism, and it is an escapable certainty that it is also the simplistic but driving force behind the hard line our culture takes regarding American English being the only dialect for all nationalities in our country. The fact of the matter is that Standard English has no greater advantages over nonstandard English, other than giving, as Beth Newman says, "undeniable social, political, and economic advantages (281)." And we all agree that a lack of using English effectively will shut off opportunities as essential as one's employment and financial legacy.

Newman believes an injustice would transpire if we follow a strident contingent's desire to be excluded from learning the prevalent standard. As was noted at the beginning of this book, a great injustice was almost delivered to one woman because of the perceptions nonstandard dialects illicit in this country. There are many who advocate the acceptance of nonstandard dialects because they refuse to be masked by the language conventions of white society, that those who would force this upon them are racists. One essayist took on this premise, head on:

> I eventually came to the conclusion that people from a residual form of primary oral culture needed to learn the surface forms of the standard grammar of a literate language to a certain extent in order to develop their own literate thought... I claim that is an expression of anti-white racism to identify Standard English with whites and to argue from this putative linkage...that it would be racist to require non-white students to learn Standard English. Standard English is race-neutral or race-independent in the sense that whether or not one can learn it does not depend on one's race (669).

Thomas Farrell makes some good points; it is really only about a person's willingness to invest in what Standard English can provide that is necessary in order to be reasonably versed in it. But there are two points I would contend. Firstly, because something is *race-neutral* does not necessarily mean that it is not biased. Christopher Jencks says that race-neutrality can be either conditional or unconditional. Unconditional race-neutral language sounds benevolent, but it is actually the most likely to perpetrate racism. "By this criterion," it is said, "teachers who are unbiased expect the same, on average, of black and white students" (275), and while it is inconclusive that real-life scenarios in classrooms will present similar results on average, clinical studies show that teachers who preach race-neutrality in their teaching (as was corroborated by Juby in Chapter 2) are the very ones most likely to fall victim to believing stereotypes about minority students. Those individuals usually have had little to no day-to-day interplay with Blacks. Furthermore, those who confide using conditional race-neutral thinking about their Black students base their interaction on observable criteria for performance based on past experience with them. This is the judgment usually employed when making placement decisions about a student and can lend to a self-fulfilling prophecy (Jencks 280). Race neutrality conditioned on potential is the third rail of the ideology and it is the believed level of performance that a student can reach at their full potential. "Full potential equals demonstrated plus latent potential," Jencks says, however, "It is alleged that teachers underestimate the latent potential of blacks more than that of whites" (Jencks 281).

Farrell knows that many feel he is considered racist for his diatribe against student rights concerning curriculum, but he denies that, "I am going to discuss the charge of racism that has been leveled against those who advocate, as I do, that all students, regardless of race, be required to learn the standard surface forms of English grammar used in most books, including the standard forms of the verb 'to be.' For I maintain that this is the only truly non-racist position" (Covino 668). Farrell, however, is again mistaken. He was mistaken about his liberal invincibility, as perhaps I am for being like-minded, but he is mistaken about another matter. I would have to disagree with Farrell about his term "anti-white racism." Racism is two-pronged, it requires not only a belief that one is superior to someone because of their race, but it also has to be combined with that believer being a member of the majority culture *and* having access to the power to implement disadvantages to the minority (Katz). A person of color, therefore, cannot be a racist in America, only bigoted or prejudiced. Yet, Farrell's main point is well taken; he was simply ignorant of the nuances of what he was actually saying. What has to be taken out of the education decision is the complete and total separation of ethnicity from the question of ability. E. D. Hirsch makes what I feel is the proper summation:

> Literate culture is the most democratic culture in our land: it excludes nobody; it cuts across generations and social groups and classes...and the only available ticket to full citizenship...membership is automatic

if one learns the background information and the linguistic conventions that are needed to read, write, and speak effectively (Covino 336-338).

Revolutionary black writers are of a mind to refuse letting the unconscious and conscious control of a White, racist institution constrain their work. They feel as Hoyt W. Fuller once said, "He is not going to separate literature from life (Mitchell 200)." Addison Gayle, Jr. wrote in his 1971 book *Black Aesthetic* and his essay, "Cultural Strangulation: Black Literature and White Aesthetic" that blackness has been assigned a proscriptive symbolization through the machinations utilized in white neo-classic theory:

> The good 'Negro Novel,' we are told by Robert Bone and Herbert Hill is that novel in which the subject matter moves beyond the limitations of narrow parochialism. Form is the most important criterion of the work…whereas form, almost nonexistent in Dostoyevsky …and totally chaotic in Kafka…must take second place to the supremacy of thought and message (Mitchell 211).

In other words, it is fine for White authors to have "large moments and grandiose ideas" in their writing. It is fine for these writers to use thematic structure, but the African American writer is believed incapable of using the narrative form competently. We must learn how to be sentence constructors, "sentence-thinkers." And unfortunately, there are some within the black literary movement who align themselves with this thinking, such as Henry Louis Gates, Jr.

He is perplexed that black literature is analyzed through its themes, and feels that until it can undergo the more stringent demands of linguistic and grammarian analysis, black literature will always lack discipline. Looked at askance by the late Barbara Christian and bell hooks for their faux essentialist leanings, while all the while ingratiating the elitist White masses with their theories, Gates, and others like him such as Cornel West, are reluctant to discuss race and racism in the context of form. These men see it more beneficial to detach from telling the black experience, and simply concentrate on telling stories, much as Paul Lawrence Dunbar did. While it is good for literature written by African Americans to be scrutinized under language and grammar criteria, it is not helpful to relegate literature about the themes of the black experience to be "rough, unfinished," and undisciplined works. To them, hooks says, "critics, writers, and academics have to give the same critical attention to nurturing and cultivating our ties to black community that we give to writing articles, teaching, and lecturing " (Anderson 124).

CHAPTER SIX
Educator Demographics

We've examined and illustrated how the social mechanism of the threat of stereotype operates; we've discussed the culture of education, and we began to delve into the various ethnicities and how they are interplayed in pedagogy. This chapter is meant to further that particular discussion because the climate of reform can only be elevated through understanding how each entity is juxtaposed to one another. A microcosmic alignment of consciousness, therefore, at a local level, cannot be realized without first viewing the macrocosm of reality within the state education system. Hamilton says that one of the main reasons why test-based accountability usually misses its mark of improving student performance is that the larger domain from which the content is derived from is left out of the analysis for the students' performance (62). Edsource, along with California census figures, gives the following information for the 2003-2004 school years regarding teacher ethnicity; this year the state is mandating a new inventory be taken:

- Whites make up the majority of educators with 73.5% teachers, and that is 10% higher than their total population. White students make up 32.5% of all children in California, virtually a 2-to-1 ratio of teacher-to-student.
- White women are the majority in that total percentage with approximately 76%.
- Hispanic educators are the next largest group with 14.2%, but they make up a total of 32.4% of the state population, and their children are 46% of the school age state population. For every 3 Hispanic students there is one Hispanic teacher, statewide.
- Blacks have 4.7% representation in education, but comprise 7.4% of the state population and Black children are 8.1% of the students.

Statewide, for every 45 Black students there is a teacher who is African American.

It is felt by many that having teachers of the same race as the students they teach are really of no advantage to the students because they are all teaching relatively the same content, regardless of the color of their skin. What having an ethnically linked teacher to a student does do, however, is to perform a sociological function (Jencks 367). If one sees more of a representation of them as being the norm, proportionately, in an environment where they are learning new things, they will then engage more with the teacher in interpreting the culture they are in.

A majority of the student populace is in Southern California, and it is in this region of the state that the effect of these demographics is most felt, on a quantitative level. In my former high school the numbers didn't bode as well. Out of 3200 students there were 515 African American. Six teachers out of 135 are African American. That means that for the African American students in the school, for every 85 of them, there is a teacher who represents them ethnically. Chances are that many may not ever experience having a teacher that looks like them, teaching them. What bodes worse for them is that the content of the pedagogy used to teach and assess them is set at a standard outside the consideration of Black culture and proclivity.

Interestingly enough, in my new high school, approximately 150 miles north of Los Angeles, there is one African American teacher aide and now me, a single Black administrator, for less than 1% of the entire student population. But this is where statistically things become askew because not only does the statistical equity apply to teachers at RHS, but it also applies to administration. RHS has the African American student body reflected statistically in its teaching body and administration, and it is 90% better than the state average, and yet the question must be asked will this self-image, self-esteem issue translate to positive academic performance?

The African American population of students in Santa Maria, California is solidly middle class, with private school attendance not being unusual within the group. Most parents of RHS students have college degrees (64%) and included in that statistic are African Americans who work in the military locally, or work for a state agency. From my observations, it seems the RHS African American student body is quite hesitant to throw about any "race card" allegations, unlike THS students who are Black. But as Steele found in his studies, even with feelings of trust intact, and similar socioeconomic environments, Black students, like RHS's, score at the same test range levels of THS's population. This proves, in this instance, that money and class are not what maintains the achievement gap. It would almost seem to inescapably point towards a shift in thinking about how to affect a change for the better, but that is not what is happening at RHS. In fact, there seems to be some void of racial consciousness amongst the African American students there, at least consciousness in the radical sense.

This small African American niche here appears to feel quite well-supported and appreciated. They perhaps show Dr. King's dream becoming reality, in that they see themselves, for all intent and purpose, as being part of a student collective firstly, and being Black, secondly. And what's more, that's what they seem to believe others feel about them. What has to be raised in their value system, however, is the desire to get the opportunities in post-secondary education that their White peers get, in order to succeed. According to the statistics of Jencks and Steele, the Black RHS seniors in the 2008 school year will have 5 graduates who will complete getting a college education, and almost 25 who will not. A 20% completion rate for Blacks versus an 80% completion rates for Whites; it is without a doubt that there are tangible ramifications from the actions which occur in educational settings by virtue of the undisturbed, and nurtured, tendrils of discrimination playing out in stereotype threat upon students of color, especially African American students.

But White students witnessing this travesty, as well, seem to lose valuable and desirable traits in a world driven by a global economy and interaction. If they don't become more-or-less *anti-racist* in their personality, as well as their locus of influence amongst their peers, then the pervasion of the hidden curriculum agenda is cemented from inertia, and the reluctance to overcome the obstacle is barely realized.

Dr. Beverly Daniel Tatum, world renowned for her groundbreaking work in social psychology and her administrative leadership as president of Spelman University, suspects that White students are basically, programmed for racial insensitivity through omission: "Most introductory psychology or developmental psychology textbooks include very little mention, if any, of racial or ethnic identity development. Because racial identity is not seen as salient for White adolescents, it is usually not included in the texts. One consequence of this omission that should concern all of us is that educators all across the country, most of whom are White, are teaching in racially mixed classrooms, daily observing identity development in process, and are without an important interpretive framework to help them understand what is happening in their interactions with students, or even in their cross-racial interactions with colleagues (xv)." Dr. Daniels Tatum seems to be stating, as I did earlier, that perceptions and trust issues are, for the most part, culturally based.

While the research of this book deliberates about how African American students feel they are being represented and assessed within the English Diasporas, this is also meant to be a dialog about racial tolerance and reciprocal ethnic leadership. What benefits a person believes they can expect from having a strong sense of their racial identity needs to be examined. Their comments to this question could be used to infer attitudes that they have about race, and more importantly, if they have the inclination to speak out in a situation where their peers express racist beliefs, views, and attitudes.

This book has not come up with any answers to the issues presented, merely explored what has been written and discussed about the opposing views. What hopefully has made a difference though has been the candid treatment given the subject matter. We have investigated the need to seriously analyze the possible consequences of illiteracy; the missteps that educators take in trying to make connections through inappropriate literature; the theoretical theory behind vernacular; the rules of structure in vernacular; and the questions related to race and acquisition. The tolerance of anyone who reads this material may now somehow be adjusted because of having information at hand to explain his or her position intelligently. Frustration over not being able to explain the unknown is what can lead to intolerance.

CHAPTER 7
The Future of African American Education

As was already stated, the final analysis of this inquiry seems to point to there being a tremendous divide about what not only Black and White students achieve in school (particularly in the field of English) but that the groups also seem to be separated by divergent philosophies concerning education, as well. RHS African American students pointed this out in their survey responses: these students were not economically disadvantaged, their school was less crowded, and a larger percentage of them were academically successful. Yet, this rural group of African American students seemed more dissatisfied with the quality of their education than their peers at THS, in Los Angeles. RHS students were more prone not to trust their teachers about cultural evaluations and assessments when it related to the subject matter (English); they were more apt to discount the teacher's skills in the subject; they were more ready to claim discriminatory environments existed at the school; they were also more convinced than the THS students that White students got better grades and training because of the privilege they had from being White. This is salient because a reasonable person would assume that the inner-city youth would be more disgruntled than the rural Black student at RHS. But that is the direct opposite of what the study revealed.

Because the RHS students do not believe the system works for them, in a higher degree than the urban students, socioeconomic differences, and physical environments don't seem to be as much a factor as one would think they would be in causing the learning gap. The African American students feel there is a standardized curriculum when it comes to their assessment and training and that that culture devalues them and a lot of what they do. The statistics in my study seem to indicate that it is indeed the teacher who is making the difference in whether or not the student engages. And even if the instructor is "color blind" and does not try to perpetrate such injustice, the curriculum, and the English canon that it springs from, trumps whatever incentives or invectives the open-minded teacher has in circumventing the inequality. The canon makes no apology for the way it covers non-white subjects, and if the teacher is only repeating the canon's precepts there will be the same disassociation as if the diatribe originated with them. The only way that that teacher can come at that reticence is to vigilantly look for opportunities to right the ship. They must check and monitor reading levels and gauge reading comprehension in the texts, continually, as well as judge introspection set about by Whites about being White. Most assuredly, there are many who would gainsay that a need exists for finding out what is the matter with White people. They are a race that reigns supreme around the world. Pragmatics states that they have set the curve for achievement.

The only way a comprehensive and embedded understanding can be made in regards to improving student interaction and achievement in English and other courses is to involve all the majority members in acknowledging their responsibility in eradicating the conceptions that work against them in working effectively with people of color; among those notions can be included: blacks have to get it together before I'll do anything on their behalf; I refuse to work with angry people; I did not own slaves; I don't see color; blacks always seem to want someone to bail them out. People feeling this way do not sense any real advantage over others in their every day pursuits.

Richard Dyer says that one of the problems with debating race relations for Whites is that they are in the driver's seat as to what is and isn't raced. And Whites certainly don't see themselves as being a race—they simply are. "There is something at stake in looking at, or continuing to ignore white racial imagery. As long as race is something applied to non-white peoples, as long as white people are not racially seen and named, they/we function as a human norm. Other people are raced, we are just people." Dyer feels the "standard of humanity" that White people arrange ensures the inevitability of their being prosperous (Rothenburg 9, 12). That is not to say that every White person is successful, or if they do have any means, it is not as if they intentionally planned on stepping on the backs of minorities to gain their status; but because of the many of their numbers who did—and do just that, and that it's been done this way repeatedly for centuries, it makes the advantage achieved being indelibly engrained.

Historians are quick to point out that there were immigrants who were once slaves in American, as well as Blacks, once upon a time. What consigned slavery to blackness, however, according to Philip C. Wander in 1972, was the semiotic shifting of going from ethnicity to race in the classifying whom was subject to the "racializing" needed to put another human being under the will of another, and that occurred as the founding fathers interpreted the colonies' notions about property (Rothenberg 31). Barack Obama says in his book, *The Audacity of Hope*, that "All the Founding fathers recognized the connection between property rights and liberty (151)." Kovel is quoted in *White Privilege* (31) as saying Europeans believed no one could do better in life than to expand upon what is the very thing you can possess; and that's your self (Kovel 18). The immigrants who came later would be indentured servants, not slaves, because the newcomers shared being members of the white race. It was to these people upon whom it was conceived that the inalienable rights were inferred to, not to Blacks. It seems hegemony and politics were conjoined and the culture devised the "one drop" solution to irrevocably separate the races while yet allowing commerce to be maintained.

This has been proven out by the relationship that African Americans and Hispanics now share. It is a similar interaction as is common between most Jews and Blacks, but that is an aside to the main point. While many Whites tend to lump Mexican Americans and Hispanics together in a completely different racial caricature, however, the very homogeny rules made in colonial times makes it difficult to subordinate Latinos to a status that is parallel to Blacks, racially. The government created two new ethnic categories of Whites in 1980, according to Neil Foley (Rothenberg 55).

Hispanics and non-Hispanics gave Latin descended people the umbrella of whiteness that absolved them from the harshest treatments reserved for Blacks, during and after the Civil Rights Movement. Foley says, "To identify oneself today as 'Hispanic' is partially to acknowledge one's ethnic heritage without surrendering one's whiteness." These Latinos did not object to segregating Blacks, or that Whites were not a superior race to Blacks. This helped with their assimilation into the American culture because they embraced the principles of many White Americans "Segregation statutes consistently defined all those without African ancestry as 'whites.' Texas, for example, defined 'colored children' as persons of mixed blood descended from 'negro ancestry' for purposes of school segregation laws and defined all persons besides those of African descent as White for purposes of its anti-miscegenation and Jim Crow laws (Rothernberg 60). Americans have reinforced the color line that has denied people of African descent full participation in American democracy. In pursuing White rights, Mexican Americans combined Latin American racialism with Anglo Racism, and in the process separated themselves and their political agenda from the Black civil rights struggles of the forties and fifties (Rothenberg 62). For these reasons, I do not place Hispanics with having the same pathos in this matter as Blacks, and once again maintain my focus on African American data in relation to the present academic situation. Spanish speaking countries have pejoratives about Blacks in their language, just like Whites do, and the groups have generally estranged themselves from maintaining a symbiotic relationship with Blacks.

In their work entitled, "Making Systems of Privilege Visible", Stephanie Wildman and Adrienne D. Davis claim, "Language contributes to the invisibility and regeneration of privilege (Rothenberg 109)." This statement alone can condemn academic scholarship in the one-sided representation of its canon. What has to be discovered and weighed, however, are the nuances behind the motivations for the obfuscation. How did we form the social hierarchies that we have today? "To begin the conversation about part of a system of categorization that we use without thinking and that seem linguistically neutral. Race and gender are, after all, just words…Imagine how long you could have a discussion with or about someone without knowing her or his gender. We place people into these categories because our world is gendered (Rothenberg 110)." This speaks as to why in my survey questionings I placed statements regarding student attitude about gender and gender discrimination. My rationale was if there is any type of discrimination, then there stands a chance for racial discrimination to be occurring there, as well. Wildman and Davis continue, "Similarly, our world is also raced, and it is hard for us to avoid taking mental notes as to race. We use our language to categorize by race, particularly, if we are white, when that race is other than white…that makes it hard to see each other as whole people…these words mask a system of power, and that system privileges whiteness (Rothenberg 110)."

CHAPTER EIGHT

Student Voices

> Like a circle in a spiral
> Like a wheel within a wheel
> Never ending or beginning.
> On an ever spinning wheel
> As the images you find
> In the windmills of your mind
> (Noel Harrison)

The paths to this point in this work have come about through a synthesis of much researched aggregate and disaggregate data and information. There were no peaks and valleys in the development of the record, but rather a slow unwinding sequence of information that had to be reordered, to make sense of it, within the design of a new voice in the understanding I wished to impart. It took five years of intensive study and conjecture, as well as enlightenment, about a subject I have a passion for. Though, there have also been varying levels of events occurring within the time I began this project (both in education and within society) that directly correlate to this study; I believe the rule of thumb is that knowledge doubles every six months since hyperspace came into existence. With no such advances it might be seen as contrived, or maybe even prescient, that the candidacy of Barack Obama played out as it has. More to the point, it is intriguing that that candidacy would have the very issues embedded in it that I had already written about in this forum. More so, that they shaped the political angles in the campaign. This election, in ways both good and bad, has brought the issue of race to the front burner of dialogue on an almost daily level, as no other has.

Still, even with a all the questions and self-inquiry that pundits brought up in the last two years, my theories about the connections between stereotype threat, high stakes assessments, and hidden curriculum were still only theories until I had pertinent numbers from my study to which I could reference, and document phenomena. The hypothesis might even have been regarded as a glorified platitude had it not been for the ability to link it actual people, and not just relying on the data from other scholars and references. Fortunately, I had the opportunity to acquire such statistics, though not as extensively, or as in depth, as I had formally set out to do. In hindsight, it was good that I didn't find all subjects that I wanted, or I'd still be calculating the spreadsheets and analyzing all the variances.

At the outset of this study, teachers were going to be interviewed as well as college level instructors, alongside the high school and college students. Logistical problems, though, made it nearly impossible to have any survey conducted at all. In the original study there were to be over four hundred subjects involved, when in the end I was lucky to have gotten only thirty-two students from the high schools. Institutional faculties, both at the secondary and post-secondary levels did not want to participate; professors at the university were asked to conduct the surveys after they'd been approved (a year-and-a-half ordeal), but were noncommittal. That cut out getting college student feedback. When I found out that I then was only going to have access to high school students, I modified my plan to juxtapose my present high school (one in a rural area) and my former school in the San Fernando Valley. But there was little to no help with getting the surveys out to students from the teachers at THS, and I did not work well with the RHS faculty in being able to disseminate the surveys to them because I had to fight even being allowed to sample the students (teacher's union). I was the outsider, and generally held in distrust and disdain by everyone involved, it seemed, but the students.

Because of the length of time spent completing this project, five years, I found myself having to relocate (new job in a new area) and that further nullified any chance at organizing college students to respond to a survey. You see, after completing my graduate English coursework, the progress with my thesis lasted so long, that I was able to get another Masters, in Education, and left the classroom to become an administrator. While moving north to Santa Barbara County I only had 3 consecutive weeks of going back-and-forth to orchestrate THS students taking and handing in the survey. I passed out over 200 there and three weeks later got 17 back. Apathy, not disdain, was the enemy. At RHS, once I got the go ahead from the superintendent to conduct the study, I had to make another adjustment. The school only had 30 African American students in total. If I got 100% return from them (though unlikely) I would have almost twice the number of respondents that THS gave me, though it was an extremely higher African American population. It looked for awhile that I would have no data to base the study upon.

I therefore decided to make the survey pool be comprised of 31 students, 15 from THS and 16 from RHS. The pool had all secondary age ranges included in it, as well as classes and genders. That number, 31, is statistically insignificant, however. For a study of this kind a demographic of around 100 subjects would show more weight; in educational studies done on the state and national levels, subject populations are not considered significant unless they contain a minimum of 100 people. But that was not going to happen, so I fixated on how my demographics could still have some validity.

My concentration for the study now was to see if the perceptions I believed would be expressed would also be consistent between urban and rural African American children. If they were congruent, it would indicate my hypothesis has some basis. It would also indicate that it is the complications about race, and not class, that prevents higher achievement levels for Black students. It would also indicate that the environments that the subjects live in, and go to school in, do not influence their performance as much as the teachers who teach them English.

The students would comprise an imaginary class of African American students who are evenly divided environmentally, half from Los Angeles County and half from Santa Barbara County. The makeup of the class is similar to what any class of African American teenagers might be, however. This is very much a random sampling of individuals, who all happen to be Black. Their responses are representative of their peers at large, mostly, and inference should lean that way in reading the facts. Following, is the make-up of the fabricated classroom.

There are 13 females in the study and 18 males; 2 of the girls are freshman class level and 1 is a sophomore (attending RHS). There were no frosh/soph students interviewed with the survey at THS. 4 of the female test subjects were juniors and 6 were seniors. 2 of the males are freshmen boys; 7 juniors and 10 seniors fill out that group. RHS 16 students had 7 girls and 9 boys; 1 of the 5 juniors is a girl and 2 of the 6 seniors are girls, also. THS's group had 7 girl and 8 boys; 3 of the girls are juniors and 4 are seniors; 3 of THS's boys were juniors and 5 were seniors.

METHOD

Students receiving the survey were only told they were answering questions in a study about the threat of stereotype. The survey contained 27 statements or questions that could be responded to on a 5-point Likert scale (strongly disagree; somewhat disagree; agree; somewhat agree, strongly agree). Students were required to identify only their year in school and their gender. Responses were input into a spreadsheet with column headings for each question, as well as identifying criteria (sex, grade). Through various sorting of the data, numeric values were given to the responses on a proportional basis, according to group. Student responses were categorized in ranks that included Overall/Baseline, Male/Female, THS/RHS, Frosh/Soph, Junior, and Senior. These categories replicate within each school's area. With all the multiple counts of an individual's response in the various groups, it was found that there would be approximately 900 assorted variances possible, all ready to associate the subject's ideas to the literature I had written.

In adding up final representative percentages for a group I devised a way to replicate authentic feedback from the subject. Because this is a 5-point Likert, and uneven in its breakdown, I split the total numbers in all "agree" responses in the spreadsheet. On either side of that is a statement that shows more-or-less the respondent slightly agreeing or slightly disagreeing. By splitting the number who stated agreement with the survey statement, I was adjusting for margins of error. Final numbers showed that there were several tangential connections created and verified through the data that was reported in this way. The reporting seems to be reliable.

DISCUSSION

It is my belief, based on the research I've conducted and from an analysis of a study, that African American students by-and-large are not being equitably trained for post-secondary placement. There is evidence to support that that happens with the intention of their teachers, aided and abetted by racist content in their curriculum, both of the obvious and hidden kind. There is also evidence to support that this exists within English departments on all institutional levels, and that the phenomena can begin as early as in the student's kindergarten class. To cure this situation there has to be a drastic change in the way high school writing assessment is done as well as an extension and modification of the English canon within curriculum. Here are the results that are most salient in the report and those that speak to assertions I made earlier in the thesis body:

1. *In English classes, I believe girls get as much access to the teacher's attention as boys (Question 1).*

More than 50% of RHS students believe there is gender equality within their classrooms. RHS Boys and THS Boys have similar percentages. RHS Girls also show similar numbers, but the THS Girls feel very strongly that teachers show no preference to them. This is important because it is an adjunct perception marker. If a student believes discrimination can be because of reasons of gender, they can also be aware of discrimination occurring on basis of race.

2. *Female English teachers are more likely to support girls more than boys in their class (Question 2).*

75% RHS Boys believe that if they have a female teacher that girls in the class will get preferential treatment. 62% of girls from RHS concur. THS students are less inclined to believe that however, THS Boys having less than half (44%) agreeing; THS Girls reverberate their initial sentiment with less than a third (29%) who believe they get more support from a female teacher.

3. *Female English teachers are more likely to support boys more than girls in their class (Question 3).*

This observation reveals how having weighted survey question can draw out inferences. Female teachers are believed to show favoritism to boys by only 10% of the RHS Boys and none of the girls believed this situation occurred at all. THS Girl's also said this is something that would not happen at THS. THS Boys, however, felt by approximately a third (31%) more, three times as much as the RHS Boys, that this was the case in their school. It should not go unnoticed that this group tends to not show very strong feelings when compared to RHS. 50% of RHS and THS Boys said they believe there was gender equality in the classroom at their respective schools. But then we get these high ratios in conjunction with that very thing, refuting their original stance. This seems to show what power lies below the surface of some seemingly oblique or obligatory question. *The RHS Boys have shown that there are significant numbers of African American students who believe gender discrimination occurs with the classroom.* This then shows an opening exists for other discrimination.

4. *I learned that "masks", "suffering", and "tricksters" are themes in African American literature (Question 6).*

This is one of the most gratifying statistics that I discovered in conducting the survey. Across the board, all the students had a firm knowledge of African American literary premises. This was important because I believe to be engaged in the dialogue, the students would have to have a working knowledge of African American literary thought, and they did. Overall, 75% of all students knew the precepts of African American literature. THS was more versed, having 71% of it s girls respond correctly compared to RHS's 43%. THS Boys were slightly higher than RHS's, 56% to 50%. This means the students were engaged with a social construct of their own identities in world context. This is also an acknowledgement that public education is doing an effective job. But with that being said, still less than half the Black students who will graduate from either school will complete college, however.

5. *English teachers I've had can readily identify the features of African American literature (Question 8).*

Trust was an important issue in student performance and overall achievement. Subsequently, trust lends to satisfaction with the entire education experience. One of the obstacles the White teacher would have to overcome would be that some of the African American students doubting their authority to teach them about literature attributed to African Americans. 79% of THS Girls felt there teachers were practiced enough in teaching to give the class; 60% of RHS Girls trusted their teachers as much; 57% of THS Boys correlated to RHS Girl sentiment about teacher competency; RHS Boys were least inclined (38%) to feel their English teachers were competent enough to teach them African American Literature.

6. *Students should be able to expect that writing about the "Black Experience" will be appreciated by any teacher, so long as it goes along with an assignment (Question 12).*

66% of RHS students believe they are allowed to write about the Black experience in the context of an assignment, and are encouraged to do so. RHS girls are an even higher number (84%). Only 43% of THS Girls felt that this was acceptable at THS

7. *Teachers want my cultural views when I'm writing about what I read (Question 16).*

This is interesting. High degrees of RHS African American females think their teachers approve that they express about themselves culturally within an assignment. They know that they are allowed to do so. When given such opportunity though, only 17% of RHS Girls would be inclined to do so. 30% of THS and RHS Boys would make any mention, and again, only 43% of THS Girls said they would use that information. What is it that prohibits such a large proportion of the students to not include African American self-referencing in their writing? I believe this shows the subgroup with the study that has recorded its first feelings about the effect of the threat of stereotype in their schooling. These students feel that if they write about themselves in a designated conveyance, (i.e., an African American) that it will either not be appreciated or it will not get them the grade they want to get from the teacher.

8. *I've never had a Black English teacher explain the importance of African American literature to me (Question 14).*

Almost 75% of RHS students have never had an African American English teacher, boys being less likely than girls. THS Girls had the lowest subgroup in this question, having only 7% of them never being taught by a Black teacher for an English class. This number is circumspect, however, due to the much high number of THS boys. 56% of THS Boys say they have never had a Black teacher in an English class while 64% of RHS Girls reported the same.

9. *I believe that students of color may receive lower grades for comparable or better work in English composition than White students (Question 19)*

25% of RHS students believe that the work of a Black student does not get assessed as highly as the work of White students. None of the RHS Girls held this view, contrary to THS Girls, 29% of whom felt this to be true. Overall, THS students weren't as convinced of this happening at THS and held at 20% believing disparity existed. 55% of RHS Boys said this was true at their school. THS Boys, however, had the second highest percentage of believers with 38% saying it was true. In only one category, was it a majority viewpoint, but there are appreciable numbers of African American students perceiving this situation to be existing.

10. Peer evaluating is a valuable tool in writing and can help prevent unfair grading (Question 20).
As a teaching strategy 25% of the students overall believe that collaborative work and peer-review can help from work being unfairly assessed. When it breaks down into subgroups, however, a spike develops. 55% of RHS Boys overall believe peer review is good and even more of the girls do at RHS (75%). THS's breakdown runs high also, 86% of the girls and 55% of the boys.

11. European American English teachers are likely to slant class subject matter to make African Americans seem inferior (Question 21).
Over 50% of the RHS students feel that English teachers slant representations of African American characters in derogatory ways. 33% of the RHS Girls subscribe to these feelings, as well. THS Girl's numbers match the overall student response, at 50%. The THS Boys spike the board with a jump to 63% of them feeling this occurring.

12. European American English teachers are not aware when they slant class subject matter to make African Americans seem inferior (Question 21).
THS students firmly believe this is happening. Only 20% of them give the teacher the benefit of the doubt and believe they do it unconsciously. THS Girl numbers are rather low as well, about 33%. RHS numbers, however, show a contrast with 56% of the Boys and 70% of the Girls feeling this not at all intentional.

13. Schools in the city make it easier to get better grades in English than they do in the suburbs (Question 23).
About a third of the RHS students feel that education is better in the suburbs and rural areas as compared to the cities. Overall, 43% of THS High students felt this. 43% of THS Girls are feeling this way, as well. But THS Boys didn't believe there was much difference, if any. They held at 20% of them believing rural education was superior.

14. African American students are encouraged to enroll in English AP classes (Question 24).
Less than half of all the students felt that African American students were encouraged to enroll in advanced placement classes.

15. *Reading is more important to my parents than it is to me (Question 26).*
High numbers of the groups did not feel enamored with the process of reading—anything. Over 50% of the RHS students, and the same from THS, felt reading was more important to their parents than it is presently to them. 67% of RHS Boys feel this way and 33% of the girls do. Similarly, THS has 69% of its boys concurring, and 29% of its girls. This is indicative of the problem in trying to bridge any gap.

16. *Reading is more important in college than it is in high school (Question 27).*
60% of all students believe that reading skills are more needed in college than they are in high school. 80% of RHS Boys and 25% of RHS Girls take that stance. There is parity with the THS responses with male and female subgroups matching the overall ration of 60%.

PROBLEMS

Lack of cooperation with educators

There was not much embracing from any educators towards the project they were asked to participate in. Though it was explained to them fully by consent advisement, they overwhelmingly denounced the investigation. The study was approved at THS by its administration, and the paperwork was placed into the entire English department office mailboxes. Not one person called to raise objection or question. I left several (24) extra copies of all the materials for the staff surveys in the school's English department chair's mailbox. Instructions had been given to turn in completed surveys to the main office, where I would pick them up. I only got 2 surveys from any of the teachers. I asked the department chair if he had the surveys I'd given him and he looked at me blandly and said he knew nothing about it. The English department at RHS is chaired by a teacher who had a conflict in personality with me and no help could be expected from her, either; in fact, when the superintendent in Santa Maria approved me handing out the surveys to the students, there were concerns raised to others in the school administration from English teachers. I therefore decided it was best to just the drop teachers quotient out of my analysis, altogether. At the post-secondary level it had been trying to get logistics and support arranged in order to have involved university students. Added to the predicament was the fact that I had moved to an area of the state more than 125 miles from the CSUN campus. I could not get approval of the survey materials completed in a time to where I would then be able to have access to African American students. There had been little communication from scholars that I did not instigate in my repeated overtures with assistance with the project.

Reading comprehensibility

Though the survey materials were constructed with the aid of professors and refined through the instructions of the Office of Research and Sponsored Projects, the survey proved a little too dense; some students needed elucidation about certain statements they were to respond to. This could be problematic for an evaluator because the survey results could then become skewed if enough students were having difficulty. Weighting certain questions to make extended inferences, however, along with the splitting of the median results from the survey's neutral ranks, hopefully has kept the margin of errors within no more than 5%.

Protocol paperwork hampers subject involvement

Statistics showed that a large percentage of students don't care to read. I believe that all the pages of explanation and consents having to be read before they could fill out the survey had many students (and maybe their parents) too fatigued to want to complete it. I believe the protocols directly affected the lack of participation in the study. What this book hopefully illustrates in regards to this, again, is that having the information is not enough. A person must be willing to use it. And in the next section, not only must they (students and teachers) be willing to digest that information, they also must be willing to hear what other students are saying about the subject, and then use that conversation as a filter for how they teach.

CHAPTER 9
Case Studies

My teacher has some sort of dislike for me, and I, as well as the rest of the class notices it. For example, during class; the whole class was to be given handout sheets to study for a test...My teacher gave every student a handout but me. She walked right past me to give it to the student next to me, and I noticed this so I decided to wait and see if maybe she needed more copies, or something. She asked me what I was doing because while I waited I decided to work on another assignment, and so I told her she never gave me anything to work on. She then asked me why I never told her to give me one, and I stated I did not know I had to if the rest of the class never had to ask...She smiled, laughed, and then sarcastically said, "Oh, puhleez—whatever." Here is a second recounting given by the same student about the same teacher: *I was absent one day because of illness and my English class got to do a large extra credit assignment. When I returned the following Monday and heard about it I asked if I could do it, since I was sick and unaware of it, and she told me 'no'. At the end of class I asked her how she saw it fair and equal that I am deprived the right to do extra-credit work that my peers all could, and she was offended greatly at my question. So, she purposefully rolled her eyes at me, let out a sigh of frustration (for the fact I was confronting her about it) and rudely pushed by me to walk away. Although these incidents are more of a personal level than a racial one, it is still not right that these things happen at all."*

Some readers may be puzzled as to why this excerpt would be placed in the body of this work at all because it is not an anecdote from a Black student. Although, one would have to admit that until the reader gets to the last few lines, they'd probably not think that this would come from a White student. That it does, however, proves one of the assertions made in Paula S. Rothenberg's book, *White Privilege*. Allan Johnson says in his article, "Privilege as Paradox" that this student was upset from her white privilege being rescinded: "Regardless of which group we're talking about, privilege generally allows people to assume a certain level of acceptance, inclusion, and respect in the world, to operate within a relatively wide comfort zone. Privilege increases the odds of having things your own way, of being able to set the agenda in a social situation and determine the rules and standards and how they're applied. Privilege grants the cultural authority to make judgments about others and to have those judgments stick. It allows people to define reality and to have prevailing definitions of reality fit their experience. Privilege means being able to decide who gets taken seriously, who receives attention, which accountable to whom and for what. And it grants a presumption of superiority and social permission to act on that presumption without having to worry about being challenged…Whiteness is privileged in this society and I have access to that privilege only when people identify me as being to the category 'white'…In similar ways, you can lose privilege if people think you don't belong to a particular category…It's important to point out that belonging to a privileged category that has an oppressive relationship with another isn't the same as being an oppressive person who behaves in oppressive ways. That whites as a social category oppress people of color as a social category, for example, is a social fact. That doesn't, however, tell us how a particular white person thinks or feels about particular people of color or behaves toward them. This can be a subtle distinction to hang on to, but hang on to it we must if we're going to maintain a clear idea of what oppression is and how it works (Rothenberg 117, 121)."

The student in this initial case study was more forthcoming with me when I interviewed her further about this incident. Being a disciplinary dean at the time I looked at her academic records and found her to be a C+/B- student; probably one who could do better, but also one who believed her privileged agenda and intelligence could let her put aside the hard work needed to excel. Her skills in English were competent, and in most campuses she would have a seat in advanced English. But, she was a junior who didn't have the sponsorship required for that. What she did have was a strong opposition to the English teacher because of perceived unfairness towards her. I asked the girl if she treated anybody else in the class this way.

"What do you mean?" she asked.

"You know, does she only give boys a hard time, or certain girls, or even races?"

"I guess it's a lot like how the black kids in class get treated."

Here is how another student recounted the feeling of the threat of stereotype being played out in their classroom over successive days. A fight eventually resulted from the non-resolution of the consternation between the two students: *The situation started probably the first week of school. The teacher was asking me a question directed personally to me. I responded to the question and **** replied with something (I'm not sure what) but he was not involved in the conversation and he rudely interjected and unnecessary comment…something to the extent of, or close to, 'Shut the fuck up'. The teacher then calmed the situation down and I thought that was the end of that. But later on, I think in the same week, I was* *talking to my friend during a free time and I notice that he is listening in on what we were talking about. Nothing else happened. Then Monday, I am doing my work and had a feeling that somebody was looking at me, and sure enough, it was****. So, I ask him, 'What are you looking at?' and he replied with 'Nothing much', and he was looking in my eyes with a threatening stare. I returned to doing my work when it happened again but I do not respond. On Tuesday, the same thing happens once more, but now he is sitting right in front of me. Now, today I am sitting and doing my work and I look and he is staring; I didn't say anything, but I look at the clock to how long he has been watching me but I still say nothing. I look up again and he staring and I tell him if I look up again and he is still staring at, I would fire on him. The teacher heard that and asked me if I was serious and I said, 'Yeah, watch me.' She sends me out of class."*

The unnamed student, one who I knew and had disciplined for inappropriate hyperbole and aggressive behavior towards staff and students, had many friends of all ethnicities, but he came from a wealthy family and was used to exerting privilege. Here, he used his manipulations to target a black student in a way to get them to be punished for a reaction to his antagonisms. Note how voiceless the black student continually says he feels. The pressure that the stares caused made the target unable to protest effectively.

These are like the micro-aggressions that Claude Steele talks about, the things that can occur to an African American that catches them unaware, but is done in an innocuous fashion, so as not to draw attention. Some would read the former statement about the "stare down" incident as not being related to race (as there were no epithets). I beg them to understand that this is something from the standards of the hidden curriculum at work in the class. Leonard Pitts Jr. gives a detailed explanation about feelings felt by many African Americans in situations such as what happened with the staring: "To be black in modern America," Pitts writes, "is to feel the touch of hidden hands pressing down upon you. You know they're there. Their effect is clear in government and university statistics documenting that, in terms of education, employment, housing, justice, health, and other quality-of-life indicators, people like you lag behind the nation as a whole. You know the hands are there, but when you turn around to catch them in the act of pushing you down, you encounter only white people with 'who, me?'" expressions on their faces (Rothenberg 138)." I remember getting the "evil eye" as a child, from Whites. That's a code word for the thinly veiled disdain given you by someone who dislikes you, and whenever you try to assert your impression about the incident, it is denied and trivialized by them and their peers. But the affect is completed; it does its work, nonetheless. It lets you know where you stand in their eyes. Pitts put it to words for me.

Here are two more incidents involving a African American student and an Asian American teacher, who eventually ended up accusing the student of threatening him, physically: *"After Mr. Pierce talked to Mr. _____ and settled everything, Mr. _____ walked back into class and I had just asked Cesar for the pencil Mr. _____ said, 'I don't want to hear another word from you, or you are gone.' After he said that I replied, 'I was just asking him for a pencil.'*

'Say something, one more time and I'm going to give you an "F" on your quiz.' After he said that, I replied by saying, 'You can't base my grade on me being tardy.' And he said he didn't care. I told him that what he was doing didn't make any sense and that angered him and he asked me if I wanted him to call my mother, or something of that ort. Then I said, 'Go ahead. Call her, because I did nothing wrong,' then he said, 'Well, go outside because you're not taking the quiz.' After he passed out all the quizzes to everybody he came outside and told me to call my Mom. I asked to speak to Mr. Pierce first, then he said, "Can you please call your mom?"

So, I called my mom on my cell phone and when I was taking to her I said, "'Mom, this teacher wants to talk to you and he is trippin'."' But it turns out she couldn't hear me, so I sad louder, "Hey, this dude in here is trippin'. He wants to talk to you.'" Then she said, "'Who?"', so I repeated the thing again, only louder. Mr. _____ heard me from inside the room and he yelled out, 'No wonder you act like that. Talking to your mom like that.' Then I said to him that I didn't disrespect my mother, it was just because she couldn't hear me on the cell phone. After that I hung up the cell phone because my mom could barely hear me. I offered to giver her number to the teacher to allow him to call her but the teacher said he'd rather send me to the dean's office.

The student then was refusing to leave the room and I had to be called back to extricate him without an assault occurring. Apparently, the teacher had said more inflammatory things regarding the student's upbringing and the teen had been pushed beyond the point of endurance. The final case study involves a female African American student from THS who had been sent to see me in the dean's office. Our procedure in the office was to have students answer five questions on a form. It is an aid in forming questions for the interview. This situation was also played out publicly in the class and then, in a sinister turn, privately. In fact, what the teacher did could have been bordering on sexual harassment or false imprisonment: *I was in my second period class and we were supposed to be watching a movie after we were done with the bell assignment. But everybody was being loud so the teacher collects our work one minute after the tardy bell rang, so of course, no one was done. When she was passing the papers back I saw that the others had gotten credit but when I got mine back I got a zero. So, I asked her why, and I was noticing at the same time that other people did the same amount of work as me. So, I asked her why I was getting a zero but I know I was wrong. So, I accepted that I was getting kicked out and just got my stuff. I went to room *** and when I got there I asked the teacher where I should sit and I followed his direction and sat down. The teacher gave his class some work to do and he comes over to me and is talking low so I am the only one who can supposedly hear him, and he is muttering, 'I know exactly why you're being sent her.' And this was before I had said anything at all. At this point, I just put my head down. He went back to teaching his class and then the bell rang. I didn't try to leave until he dismissed his class. I was walking out he blocks the door and I accidentally bump into him because I didn't think he was standing there intentionally. Then he's stepping towards me,* *all in my face, and I asked him to nicely back up a little bit, about 3 times. He said, 'I know you're feeling uncomfortable. Well, I'm trying to teach you a lesson.' So, seeing that he wasn't going to do differently and he was coming towards me again,, I asked him to again back away because he was making me uncomfortable. He told me to sit down but something was telling me not to. So, I said, "You didn't even attempt to respect me when I asked you to back up." Then he said to me, 'Well, you'll be coming to my class tomorrow, and when you're in my class you are my responsibility and you have to do what I say.' He was all up on me, pointing his finger in my face and when he created an opening I walked out of his classroom. I was unsure if I should have done that, or not, but that was the only thing that came to mind at the moment. I was so uncomfortable.*

This incident, though incendiary, was not the worst of things that happen in LAUSD. In fact, the statistics in this study are so compelling because to my knowledge, the RHS students didn't report nearly as heinous events happening to them, yet their feelings were much more irritated than these THS students, who, as you can now see, are experiencing some outrageous methodology in teaching from the school. This last scenario is wrong on so many different levels that it is hard to know where to begin. First of all, we need to set up the premise about the student. She had a disciplinary history of being disruptive and uncooperative in class. Tardiness was also a major problem, along with low production. The student's English teacher is White, and the student is running rough-shod over her sometimes. But the class is early in the day. I could understand if this was right after lunch or the final period, but a teacher should be fresh enough to handle a difficult student in a second period class. Instead, the teacher talks to a colleague, a male colleague, and asks him to take her on a couple days to straighten her out. She didn't send her to a female teacher because she was sure the same results would come about in that class as it had in hers.

The male English teacher, hearing a friend and colleague is having problems with a difficult student wants to do the male thing and "fix" the problem, or neutralize the situation from happening again, or as much. He volunteers to give her some "old school" training to whip her into shape. When the girl came late to class that day her teacher already had everything worked out. The problem that arises is that she punished her with a grade for her attitude and attendance, which is illegal. Then when the teacher is called on this irregularity she casts the child off to a new road of perdition down the hallway. I don't know where that teacher came from, but from reading the student's report I couldn't help but envision the old Southern ploy of harassing female slaves and how they were toyed with; The incident the girl unfolds just smacks of racist underplay in the guise of collegial assistance. Now, place yourself mentally in this child's situation. She has had a man break areas of trust and confidentiality, as well as invade her privacy. He even admitted that he knew what he was doing was probably making her feel uncomfortable, and that is simply a sadistic taunt to a child. What would have happened had she sat down in a desk? That night she has to go home and think about what awaits her tomorrow morning in 2nd period. More than likely she will ditch the class in order not to put herself in a precarious situation. As a parent, how would you feel if that happened to your daughter?

Tim Wise would like it brought to mind how many White kids in that class didn't have to put up with that intimidation, "When we hear about things like racial profiling, we think of it in terms of what people go through, never contemplating what it means for whites and what we don't have to put up with. We might know that a book like *The Bell Curve* denigrates the intellect of Blacks, but we ignore the fact that in so doing, it elevates the same in Whites, much to our advantage in the job market and schools, where those in authority will likely view us as more competent than persons of color. That's what keeps people of color off-balance in a racist society; that is what keeps whites in control: a truism that must be discussed if whites are to understand our responsibility to work for change. Each thing with which 'they' (Blacks, "others") have to contend with as they navigate the waters of American life is one less thing whites have to sweat: and that makes everything easier, from finding jobs, to getting loans, to attending college…As to why we should want to end racial privilege—aside from the moral argument—the answer is straightforward; the price we pay to stay one step ahead of others is enormous. In the labor market, we benefit from racial discrimination in the relative sense, but in absolute terms, this discrimination holds down most of our wages and living standards by keeping working people divided and creating a surplus labor pool of 'others' to whom employers can turn when the labor market gets tight or workers demand too much in wages or benefits. We benefit in relative terms from discrimination against people of color in education, by receiving, on average, better resources and class offerings. But in absolute terms, can anyone deny that the creation and perpetuation of miseducated persons of color harms us all? And even disparate treatment in the justice system has its blowback on the white community. We may think little of the racist growth of the prison-industrial complex, as it snares far fewer of our children. But considering that the prisons warehousing black and brown bodies compete for the same dollars needed to build colleges for everyone, the impact is far from negligible. In California, since 1980, nearly 30 new prisons have opened compared to two four-year colleges, with the effect that the space available for people of color and whites to receive a good education has been curtailed…or contingents of white parents, speaking out in a school board meeting against racial tracking in class assignments: a process through which kids of color are much more likely to be placed in basic classes, while whites are elevated to honors and advanced placement, irrespective of ability. Protesting this kind privilege—especially when it might be working to the advantage of one's own children—is the sort of thing we'll need to do if we hope to alter the system we swear we're against…And we must protest the privileging of elite, white male perspective in school textbooks. We have to demand that the stories of all who have struggled to radically transform society be told: and the existing texts don't do that, we must dip into our own pockets and pay for supplemental materials that teachers could use to make the classes they teach meaningful. And if we're in a position to make a hiring decision, we should go our way to recruit, identify and hire a person of color. What these suggestions have in common—and they're hardly an exhaustive list—is that they require whites to leave the comfort zone to which we have grown accustomed. They require time, perhaps money, and above all else, courage; and they ask us to focus a little less on the relatively easy, though important, goal of 'fixing' racism's victims (with a bit more money for this or that, or a little more affirmative action), and instead to pay attention to the need to challenge and change the perpetrators of and collaborators with the system of racial privilege." And Rothenberg goes further to add, "And those are the people we work with, live with, and wake up to every day. It's time to revoke the privileges of whiteness (Rothenberg 133-136)."

In concluding this writing, I would have to say that the journey has not been without much growth in my personal skills as a writer because of the training I received in the halls of academia. Paired with that gift, however, was a responsibility to examine my life and the conditions of others and to do things to make smooth the way for those who follow behind me, while simultaneously giving voice to the voiceless yet today. And then even with all ideological goodwill presented in summation, there are moments that rock me back to incredulity of the task before us all. And it can become somewhat comical, through a possible over-analyzing of circumstances.

As I was running a final sweep over the last 30 or so pages of the thesis with the grammar tool in my word processing program, the computer highlighted the contraction "I'm" somewhere. I knew that it was used correctly, but right-clicked on the word to clear the error. The suggestion given by the computer was to change the word from "I'm" to "I are", something that is non-grammatical and possibly Ebonics. Now, I know that some of the tools Microsoft uses with its programs have limitations (it can't differentiate homonyms or synonyms when used in certain contexts and it omits the corrections) but there is an uncanny and somewhat creepy anecdote that this reverberates with in an article previously mentioned.

In "Crazy Sometimes" Lenard Pitts recounts how some unidentified reader sent him an email that revealed what she felt was a sinister conspiracy set up by a racist programmer in her computer's word processing program (Rothenberg 139). She told Pitts to type in the sentence "I'd like all Negroes to die", highlight it, and apply the thesaurus tool. The woman said he would see "I'll drink to that". Well, Pitts did as she said and indeed, the affirmation did come up. But he did some further investigating and came to see by inputting several different and even non-racial declarations, that the same response would be produced. Any sentence starting with "I'd like…" would get the "glitch" to occur. The woman still didn't hold to what Pitts said to her in rejoinder, "Somehow, she was still convinced a software maker had it in for black folks, but I was too naïve to understand the machinations of the white man's conspiracy."

Microaggressions Across the Great Divide

Now, I tended to believe, along with Pitts, that there was some delusional apprehension evident in the allegations that that woman made. Heck, I couldn't even get my laptop to produce the glitch; but when I had my own computer supply me with a suggested correction to use Ebonics in my document, well, now I'm not so sure. In an earlier version of this book I once said that African Americans are a schizophrenic race of people. I was being somewhat facetious then, but now I feel freer to lay that claim after someone else has already said in public record that my race is crazy sometimes. A-hem, excuse me. Could you assist me? It seems I've had my first micro-aggression for the day.

WORKS CITED

Adams, Peter Dow. "Basic Writing Reconsidered." <u>Journal of Basic Writing</u> 21.1.: 1993. 22-35.

Akmajian, Adjian, Ed. <u>Linguistics: An Introduction to Language and Communication</u>. Cambridge: MIT Press. 2001.

Anderson, Walter Truett. <u>The Truth About The Truth: De-confusing and Re-constructing the Postmodern World</u>. New York: Putnam. 1995. 18, 124.
    hooks, bell. "Postmodern Blackness". <u>Yearning: Race, Gender, and Cultural Politics</u>. Boston: South End Press. 1990. 23-31.
    Kvale, Steinar. "Themes of Postmodernity" <u>Psychology and Postmodernism</u>. Sage Publicatons, Inc.

Appiah, Kwame Anthony. Biographical note. <u>Narrative of the Life of Frederick Douglass, an American Slave & Incidents in the Life of a Slave Girl</u>. New York: Random House. 2000. xi-xvi.

Anonymous. "Educating Black Students." <u>Education Digest</u>. May. Vol. 61, Iss. 9: 1996. 31-36. "The Condition of Education 1994." 1, 15, 49, 149 and "The Condition of Education 2000" (Table 32-1), (Table 32-3).

Arnett, C., J. Dailey-O'Cain, R. Lippi-Green, and R. Simpson. "Teaching children how to discriminate: standard language ideology and the perpetuation of linguistic stereotypes through Disney's animated films." Poster presentation, <u>New Waves of Analyzing Variation (NWAVE)</u> Stanford University. 1994. 93-94.

Bruna, Liza, et al. "Assessing Our Assessments: A Collective Questioning of What Students Need—and Get." <u>Journal of Basic Writing</u> 17.1, 1998. 73-95.

CCCC Executive Council. "Writing Assessment: A Position Statement." CCCC Position Statement. 1995.

Clark, Steve February 1965, The Final Speeches: Malcolm X. New York: Pathfinder. 1992. 37-38, 265, 266.

Covino, William A. and David A. Joliffe Rhetoric: Concepts, Definitions, Boundaries. Boston: Allyn and Bacon. 1995. 336-338, 593, 668
    Farrell, Thomas J. "A Defense for Requiring Standard English." PRE/TEXT 7. 165-179. Arlington: University of Texas.
    Hirsch, E. D. Jr. "The Decline of Teaching Cultural Literacy." Cultural Literacy. New York: Houghton Mifflin. 1987.
    Pike, Kenneth. "Language as Particle, Wave, and Field." The Texas Quarterly 2.2. 1959. 37-54.
    Donald, Janet and D. Brian Denison. "Evaluating Undergraduate Education: The Use of Broad Indicators." Assessment & Evaluation in Higher Education: March, Vol. 21, Issue 1: 23. 1996.
    Dyson, Michael Eric, Is Bill Cosby Right? (Or Has The Black Middle Class Lost Its Mind?). New York: Basic Civitas. 2005. 6.
    April 4, 1968: Martin Luther King Jr's Death and How It Changed America Forever. New York: Basic Civitas. 2008. 229.

Eagleton, Terry. Literary Theory: an introduction. 2nd ed. Minneapolis: University of Minnesota Press. 2001. 87-88. Peirce, C. S., father of American semiotics.

Ethnic Notions. DVD video. Dir. Marion Riggs. Prod. Vivian Kleiman. Narrator. Esther Rolle. California Newsreel. 1987.

Freel, Ann. "Achievement in Urban Schools: What Makes the Difference?" Education Digest. Vol. 64, Iss. 1: 1998. 17.

Gadda, George and Faye Peitzman. With Different Eyes: Insights into Teaching Language Minority Students Across the Disciplines. Reading: Addison-Wesley Publishing Company. 1994.

Gallagher, Donald and Don Bagin and Edward H. Moore. 8th Ed. The School and Community Relations. Boston: Pearson Publishing. 2005.

Grayson, Dolores and Dolores Martin. 3rd Ed. GESA Teachers Handbook. San Francisco: Graymill. 1995.

Grant-Thompson, Sheila K. and Donald R. Atkinson, "Cross-Cultural Mentor Effectiveness and African American Male Students." Journal of Black Psychology, Vol. 23. No. 2, May. 1997. 120.

Gupta, Abha. "What's up wif Ebonics, Y'all?" Internet: academic journal article. http://www.readingonline.org/articles/gupta. 1997.

Hamilton, Laura S., Stephen P. Klein and Brian M. Stechler. Making Sense of Test-Based Accountability in Education. Internet: academic book. 2002. http://rand.org/pubs/monograph_reports/MR1554/.

Harley, Kay, and Sally I. Cannon. "Failure: The Student's or the Assessment's". Journal of Basic Writing 15.1: 75 1996.

Helmers, Marguerite. Ed. Intertexts: Reading Pedagogy in College Writing Classrooms. Mahwah, NJ: Lawrence Erlbaum Associates, Publishing. 2003. 197, 201, 214.
    Steedman, Carolyn Kay. Landscape for a Good Woman. New Brunswick, NJ: Rutgers University Publishers. 1987. 1440.

Hjortoshi, Keith. The Transition to College Writing. Boston: Bedford/St. Martin's. 2001. 3, 13, 82.

Jencks, Christopher and Meredith Phillips, Ed. The Black-White Test Score Gap. Brookings Institute Press. Washington, D.C.; 1998. 67-68, 83, 274, 275, 276, 280, 281, 329,337, 340-342, 376, 380, 392.
    Braddock, Jomills II, and Robert E. Slavin. "Why Ability Grouping Must End: Achieving Excellence and Equity in American Education." Journal of Intergroup Relations. Vol. 20. No. 2. 1993. 51-64.
    Lightfoot, Sarah. Worlds Apart: Relationships between Families and Schools. Basic Books. 1978. 85.
    Scott Gregory, Sophronia. "The Hidden Hurdle". Time. 1992. 44-46.
    Steinberg, Laurence, Sanford Dornbusch, and Bradford Brown. "Ethnic Differences in Adolescent Achievement: An Ecological Perspective." American Psychologist. Vol. 47. No. 6. 1992. 728.
    Swidler, Ann. "Culture in Action: Symbols and Strategies." American Sociological Review 51: 1986. 273-86.

Jordan, Winthrop. White Over Black: American Attitudes Toward the Negro 1550-1812. The University of North Carolina Press. Chapel Hill. 1969. 229.

Juby, Heather L. "The Relationship Between Racism and Racial Identity for White Americans: A Profile Analysis". Journal of Multicultural Counseling and Development. 2004. 9.

Katz, Judith. White Awareness. Norman: University of Oklahoma. 1978. 51.
Kennedy, Randall. nigger: The Strange Case of a Troublesome Word. New York: Vintage Books. 2002.

Leitch, Vincent B. and Eds. The Norton Anthology of Literary Theory and Criticism. New York: W.W. Norton & Company. 2001: pg. 765, 875, 1150, 1153, 1391, 2425, 2431-2432;

    Baker, Houston A. "Blues, Ideology, and Afro-American Literature." Chicago: University of Chicago Press. 1984.

    Gates, Henry Louis Jr. "Talking Black: Critical Signs of the Times." Loose Cannons: Notes on the Culture Wars. 1992.

    Hurston, Zora Neale. "Characteristics of Negro Expression." Negro: An Anthology. 1970.

    Marx, Karl. "Economic and Philosophic Manuscripts of 1844." Manifesto of the Communist Party. 1932.

    Nietzsche, Friedrich. Ed/trans., Speirs, R. "On Truth and Lying in a Non-Moral Sense." The Birth of Tragedy and Other Writings. Cambridge: Cambridge University Press. 1999.

    Wimsatt, W.K. "The Affective Fallacy." Sewanee Review. (Winter 1949). University of the South. 1946.

Linn, Michael D. and Linda Miller-Cleary. Linguistics for Teachers. New York: McGraw-Hill. 1993. 118.

McCormick, Kathleen. The Culture of Reading & the Teaching of English. Manchester: Manchester University Press. 1994.

McMichael, G. and Editors, Anthology of American Literature: Vol. 1, 4th ed. New York: McMillan Publishing Company: 1989. 629, 632.

McNenny, Gerri. Mainstreaming Basic Writers: Politics and Pedagogies of Access. Mahwah, NJ: Lawrence Erlbaum Associates. 2001.

Margolis, Eric. "Class Pictures: Representations of Race, Gender and Ability in a Century of School Photography". Tempe: Educational Policy Archives. Internet: http://:www.epaa@asu.edu. Vol. 8. No. 31. 2000.

    Detroit Photographic Company. Detroit Publishing Collection. Internet: http://www.memory.loc.gov/ammem/detroit/detcoll.html/.

    Jackson, Philip. Life in the Classroom. New York: Teachers Press. 1968.

    New York Public Library Schomburg Center for Research in Black Culture: Digital Schomburg: http://digital.nypl.org/schomburg/images_aa19/.

    The Hidden Curriculum in Higher Education. New York: Routledge-Falmer. 2001.

    Turner, P. A. Ceramic Uncles and Celluloid Mammies: Black Images and Their Influence on Culture. New York: Anchor Books. 1994.

Mitchell, Angelyn. Within the Circle: an anthology of African American Literary Criticism from the Harlem Renaissance to the present. London: Duke University Press. 1994. 135, 139, 200, 211.

Ellison, Ralph. "Twentieth Century Fiction and the Black Mask of Humanity". From Shadow and Act. New York: Random House. 1964.

Fuller, Hoyt W. "Towards a Black Aesthetic." The Critic. Vol. 26. No. 5. 1968.

Gayle, Addison Jr. "Cultural Strangulation: Black Literature and White Aesthetic." The Black Aesthetic. New York: Doubleday. 1971.

NBC Television. Interview. Dateline. New York: NBC Studios, 28/5/2004.

NBC Television. Interview. Meet The Press. New York: NBC Studios, 23/3/2008.

NBC Television. News Article. Nightly News. New York: NBC Studios, 01/4/2008.

Newman, Beth S. 2nd Ed. Teaching Students to Write. New York: Oxford University Press. 1995.

Orfield, Gary and Chungmei Lee. "Brown At 50: King's Dream or Plessy's Nightmare?" Internet: http://www.civilrightsproject.harvard.edu/research/reseg04/brown50.pdf. 2004.

Perry, Mary. 2005. "Resource Cards on California Schools." Selected Readings on California School Finance. Palo Alto: Edsource, Inc.

Ruenzel, David. "Training Days". Internet: interview. Teacher Magazine. Vol. 17, No. 1. 58-59. http://www.edweek.org/tm/articles. 2005.

Schroeder, Ken. "Black Males' Motivation." Education Digest. Jan.. Vol. 63, Iss. 5: 1998. 73.

Soitos, Stephen. The Blues Detective: A Study of African American Detective Fiction. Amherst: University of Massachusetts Press. 1996.

Steele, Claude, M. Thin Ice: 'Stereotype Threat' and Black College Students. The Atlantic Monthly. Vol. 284, No. 2. 1999. 44-54.

Tchudi, Steven N. and Susan J. 2nd Ed. The English Language Arts Handbook: Classroom Strategies for Teachers. Portsmouth: Boynton/Cook Publishers. 1999.

Thompson, Gail. Through Ebony Eyes. New York: Jossey-Bass. 2004.

Tim Wise. "White Privilege and its Effect on Film and Television". Address. Meeting of Los Angeles Television Writers Guild and Screen Actors Guild. Los Angeles. 21 January 2006.

Winsboro, B and I. D. Solomon. "Standard English vs. 'the American dream'." Education Digest: 1990. 51-52.